THE PETRIFIED WOMAN

by
PETER BUTT

Blackwattle Press
Sydney, Australia
www.blackwattlepress.com.au
Copyright © Peter Butt 2023
Copyright © 2023 Blackwattle Press Pty Limited

All rights reserved. No part of this publication may be reproduced, stored in a retrieval system or transmitted, in any form or by any means, electronic, mechanical, photocopying, recording or otherwise, without the prior written permission of the publishers and copyright holders.

A catalogue record of this book is available at the National Library of Australia

Butt, Peter, 1954-
The Petrified Woman

ISBN: 978-0-6457318-0-4

1. True Crime - Australia. 2. Australia - History.
Publisher: Peter Butt
Associate Publisher/Editor: Sarah Staveley
Design: Blackwattle Press
Cover Images:
Website: www.blackwattlepress.com.au

ABOUT THE AUTHOR

Peter Butt is an Australian investigative filmmaker specialising in true crime and espionage. He has produced and directed major history series and dozens of documentary specials for local and international broadcasters. His multi-award-winning film, Who Killed Dr Bogle & Mrs Chandler?, remains the highest-rating commissioned documentary in ABC TV history.

His book on the Bogle Chandler case was shortlisted for the 2014 NSW Premier's Literary Awards - Douglas Stewart Prize for Non-Fiction. In 2022, he produced a five-part podcast series on the case.

Peter's book Merchants of Menace reinvestigates the notorious Nugan Hand bank, which was involved in gunrunning and money laundering for drug traffickers and the CIA. The book reveals new evidence about the mysterious death of the bank's CEO Frank Nugan and uncovers the new identity and whereabouts of its co-founder Michael Hand, one of the world's most elusive corporate fugitives.

CONTENTS

FLOOD	1
UNDERTAKEN	5
SHIVER	13
SUSPECT	16
HOUSEKEEPER	29
WONDERLAND	37
WRATH	46
I JUST SHOT THE MISSUS	49
THIS STRANGEST OF CRIMES	51
WITNESSES	57
MURTHOITES	66
MANIA	70
SNOOK	79
BROTHER	87
UNKNOWN-UNKNOWN	97
I'LL SHOOT MYSELF	99
CIRCUS	104
FEUD	113
BREAK POINT	119
THRUST	125
CAVE	128
ROAD TO TAREENA	131
PERSEVERE	134
AFTERWORD	141

**For
Unknown-Unknown**

CHARACTERS

Andy Peterson - Labourer, Renmark
Charles Bath - Brother of Russell Bath
Charlie Wilson - Irrigation Worker, Renmark
Constable Weston - Victoria Police
Dan O'Connell - Fisherman
Detective David Flint - South Australia Police, Renmark
Detective Inspector G. L. Gully - CIB, Adelaide
Detective John Killeen - Victoria Police
Detective L. Harper - CIB, Adelaide
Don Bruce - Witness
Dr. J. M. Dwyer - Pathologist
Eva Edge - Adelaide Resident
Harry Salter - Tramway Worker
H. H. Hobcroft - Coroner, Renmark
Humphrey Kempe - Owner Lindsay Point Station
John Breen - Lindsay Point Station Resident
Lucy Snook - Witness
Margaret Ellis (nee Salter) - Harry Salter's Daughter
Margaret Salter - De facto wife of Russell Bath
Mr Favalora - Lawyer
Mrs Alice Price - Witness
Ron Trigg - Undertaker
Russell Bath - Farm Worker Lindsay Point Station
Valda Jones - Witness
William 'Bill' Phillips - Witness
William Sleeman - Doctor, Renmark

1

FLOOD

It was September 1951. A month of rain across eastern Australia had swelled the country's longest waterway, the River Murray – a 2500-kilometre-long winding behemoth. In the northwest Victorian town of Mildura, floodwaters had washed away levee banks, destroying orchards and vegetable gardens, threatening glass houses, and turning grazing pastures into stinking, mosquito-infested swamps. Scientists feared another outbreak of encephalitis, which only the previous summer had blighted the river town for the first time in recorded history.

Fifty miles downstream in South Australia, the townspeople of Renmark were also on edge. The first wave of high water struck just after midnight on Monday, September 17. With the river rising an inch a day, all eyes were on the levee. Floodwaters had already broken through irrigation gates and submerged 21st Street. Locals reported a prevalence of snakes driven from the river flats by the rising water. One desperate snake had crawled into the cabin of a school bus that had stopped on its regular route.

The River Murray was already five feet higher than what the Engineering and Water Supply Department considered 'full'. Another five feet and the record books would be broken. Following a decade of drought, the once wilting gum trees that lined its banks were now knee-deep in whirling water. Here and there, eddies, like liquified whirlwinds, swept up logs, under-growth and soil like a voracious monster. Debris was causing havoc for professional fishermen and the paddle steamers operating between Renmark and Mildura. On Monday evening, September 24, sleeping passengers on the paddle steamer Marlon were awakened by a tremendous thud. They ran on deck in their pyjamas to discover that the unpredictable current had forced the vessel off course. She had struck a tree, and the damage took her out of service.

Early on Wednesday, September 26, 1951, thirty-nine-year-old irrigation worker Charlie Wilson set off on his boat upstream from Renmark to enjoy a day off work. That morning, the river was flowing at least five miles an hour and carrying a fair amount of debris, forcing Wilson to keep a vigilant eye out for logs.

At around eight o'clock, Wilson arrived at his favourite spot north of Woolenook Bend. He dropped anchor below the high cliffs close to the southern shore and settled in for a morning's fishing.

Professional fishermen, who held leases along this section of the river, jealously guarded their territory against greedy amateurs by spreading spurious claims that the fish had gotten wise and moved away from their patch. But Charlie Wilson knew better. Woolenook was an angler's paradise. During the last War, the army had set up a Japanese internment camp on the northern shore. After a long day of cutting timber, the internees were allowed to fish for dinner, and their efforts were rewarded with rich pickings of redfin, cod, callop and bream.

At 11.20 am, with a bucket full of cod and bream, Wilson weighed anchor and set off back to Renmark, unaware that his biggest catch was yet to come. Ten minutes downstream, a glint from the corner of his eye drew his attention. For all the world, it looked like a mannequin – the type he'd seen in department store windows in Adelaide – floating face down. With his curiosity piqued, he motored on a few hundred yards, turned back and drew close enough to prod it with his oar, causing it to bob a little out of the water. This was no mannequin but a naked human body.

'Now that's something you don't see every day,' he thought.

Wilson carefully manoeuvred the body beside his boat, tied a rope to it, and then towed it close to the riverbank, where he secured it to a tree that edged the mudflats. Fortunately, the floodwaters were opaque with red earth and hid the worst of the grisly find. He daren't touch the body, let alone turn it on its back. But as he carefully adjusted the rope, he brushed the back of his hand against the thigh, and his blood turned cold. The flesh was hard as stone.

On his way back to Renmark, Charlie Wilson rehearsed what he would say to the police.

"I went fishing and hooked a corpse!"

As flippant as it sounded, the statement was the simple truth. But shock soon set in, and Charlie was consumed by thoughts about how the poor victim might have met his or her fate.

One thing was sure - the great flood of September 1951 was not going to be forgotten around these parts for a while.

2

UNDERTAKEN

At around 3.30 pm, Detective David Flint overheard an excited male voice stumbling over his words, telling the weighty desk sergeant about finding a body in the river. Flint turned and nodded to his colleague to send the fellow over to his desk.

Wilson explained to Flint that he initially thought the body was a shop dummy.

"It was face down and had no hair, and I couldn't tell if it was a man or a woman. I secured it to a tree at the south end of the Heading property, near Woolenook Bend."

Flint looked at his watch, picked up the phone and asked the desk sergeant to put him through to Ron Trigg.

Detective David Flint

Charlie Wilson accompanied Detective Flint in a police car north along Murtho Road. Undertaker Trigg followed in his mortuary van. The bullock wagon had long since given way to the motor car. Nevertheless, travellers rarely soliloquised about the speed or comfort of driving on South Australia's outback roads, especially along this rutted track.

"This better not be a waste of time," warned Flint. "You sure you can find it from land?"

Hanging on for dear life, Wilson told Flint that he worked for the Renmark Irrigation Trust and knew the river like the back of his hand. In his years as an apprentice, the old timers had shown him where they'd moored a floating pumping plant, the Argo, at Woolenook Bend.

Charlie Wilson wondered aloud why other fishermen or the officers aboard the paddle steamers hadn't noticed the body - unless, of course, it hadn't travelled very far.

Thirty minutes out from Renmark, Wilson directed Flint onto the Heading property and down a boggy track, at the end of which lay the swollen river. Flint and Trigg donned rubber boots and gloves and followed Wilson across swampy ground to the semi-submerged tree where he'd secured the body.

The three men stood scrutinising the corpse. The most unusual aspect was the pale, waxy nature of the skin. Flint lifted the shoulder a little. The skin was taut as if it had undergone some form of petrification. He and Trigg carefully turned the body face up, revealing, to their shock, an absence of soft tissue above the nose and no eyes. Both arms were laid across the chest, but there were no hands, and both feet were devoid of toes.

'It looks to be female,' Flint suggested, though without any certainty.

Trigg returned to his vehicle and retrieved a mortuary stretcher. The three men stood silently for a moment, taking in the sad and confronting sight, before carefully manipulating the gurney under the floating body. They carried it to the mortary van. Trigg covered the corpse with a sheet and secured it with leather straps. Flint and the undertaker then slid it into the vehicle.

At the Renmark Police Morgue the following morning, Flint watched as local practitioner William Sleeman conducted a partial post-mortem examination. Only four years out of medical school, the boyish-looking doctor had mainly carried out perfunctory autopsies: heart attack and stroke victims and the occasional farm or car accident. His most distressing case to date had been a five-month-old boy who accidentally suffocated in his pram.

Mopping perspiration from his forehead, Sleeman said that he'd never seen a corpse in this abnormal, petrified condition. With bits of anatomy missing, the body resembled one of those Greek or Roman statues pictured in Readers Digest that had lain at the bottom of the ocean for thousands of years. But there were only minor indications of marine life activity upon the body, leaving Sleeman to estimate that the corpse had been immersed in water for no more than a month.

He determined that the body was that of a white female, five feet two inches high and between forty and forty-five years of age at the time of death. She had no teeth, and the gums were smooth, which suggested that she had worn dentures for at least twelve months.

Flint pointed out a fracture on the left side of the skull. Dr Sleeman stated that it had possibly contributed to the woman's death but that he would be unwilling to swear to it conclusively at an Inquest.

The South Australia Police protocol called for homicide cases to be overseen by the Criminal Investigation Branch in Adelaide. Flint called his city colleagues on the station's newly installed radio-phone. He briefed them on the discovery of the body and the findings of the post-mortem, which he said posed more questions than provided answers. His hunch was that the victim had been murdered, but identification of the body - the obvious priority - was going to be difficult.

The following day, Adelaide detective Len Harper drove to Renmark in a police van. After a briefing with Flint, he collected the body and transported it to the Police Morgue in Adelaide.

The same afternoon, David Flint and a constable set off upriver by boat to talk with landholders, farmhands and woodcutters, asking if anyone knew of a woman who'd gone missing. Flint had prepared rations and first aid kits, as they would also be heading onshore to search for a possible burial site, even though such a site likely remained submerged under floodwater. Flint knew the coroner would expect him to follow up on every possible line of enquiry.

In Adelaide, the following morning, police pathologist Dr J. M. Dwyer, who had performed 1,800 autopsies since the War, carried out a second and far more detailed post-mortem examination. Like his Renmark counterpart, Dwyer determined that the body was that of a woman, of approximately five feet two inches in height, of heavy build, weighing around eleven and a half stone, and big busted. Diamond-shaped markings on her upper right thigh suggested that she had been resting against cyclone wire or a wire mattress. He recorded that the woman had suffered a four-inch by two-inch skull fracture. There was no doubt in Dwyer's mind that she had been alive when she suffered extreme trauma to the head, perhaps caused by a fist or an instrument of some kind. He was also convinced that the woman lying on the slab had been murdered. But the next question that needed answering was her identity. With the entire tissue of her face missing, as well as her hair, hands, toes and teeth, Dwyer acknowledged that identification may prove elusive.

The most striking feature of the body was the state of the flesh, a condition Dwyer described as calcification and fatty mummification. The calcification of human bodies was rarely reported in Australia. Dwyer assumed it came about as a result of specific circumstances: she'd been buried in limestone-rich soil not exceeding 50 degrees Fahrenheit[1] for at least four months.

---

[1] 10 degrees Celsius

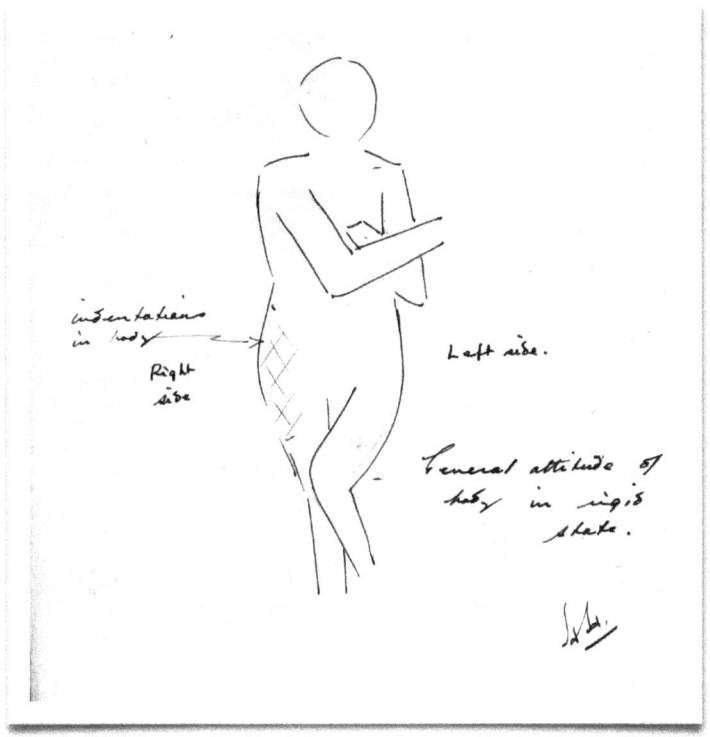

In the past, numerous killers had attempted to cover up their crimes by burying their victims in quicklime, believing that lime would completely destroy a body. But the opposite is true. While lime will cause a small amount of superficial burning, it essentially preserves bodies.

Dwyer suggested that the woman's body may not have been buried in South Australia. More likely, it was interred in a location experiencing colder temperatures, either in New South Wales or Victoria, and perhaps in alpine country. He also suspected that the burial site was likely on the bank of a river in an area with sparse vegetation, which allowed floodwaters to swirl open the grave and release the body.

In his report, he deduced that her death had occurred at least twelve months earlier, and at the latter end of summer. Therefore, she was killed between March and September 1950, twelve to eighteen months before her discovery.

Subsequent events would prove Dwyer right.

WOMAN'S BODY IN RIVER MYSTERY

MILDURA, Sun.—Police believe a woman whose body was found in the Murray River near Renmark last week died about six months ago and may have been murdered.

Despite extensive investigations in three States, her identity is not yet known, and may never be known.

Police believe she may have been murdered, because the skull and body were severely fractured.

Renmark fisherman, Charles Wilson, found the body floating in the river about 12 miles upstream from Renmark on Wednesday.

Police say that the body apparently floated down the flooded river and could have come from as far away upstream as Albury.

Adelaide pathologist, Dr. J. M. Dwyer, who conducted a second postmortem examination on the body on Saturday, said the woman had been dead six months or more.

He described her as about 5ft. 2in., of heavy build weighing between 11 and 12 st., and aged between 40 and 50 years.

Police believe the condition of the body indicates that the woman had not been in the water for the full period since she died.

They say it is likely that the body was exposed by floodwaters and washed into the river's midstream by a strong current.

None of the descriptions of women reported missing along the river more than six months ago fits that of the dead woman.

Renmark police believe the woman could have been one of the many itinerants who frequent places all along the river.

Inquiries at Renmark are being handled by Det. D. O. Flint. He is preparing a report for the Coroner (Mr. H. H. Hobscroft).

3

SHIVER

On receipt of the pathologist's report, Adelaide detectives radioed a bulletin to police stations across New South Wales and Victoria with a detailed description of the mystery woman.

Europeans were regularly fished out of the River Murray, and most were victims of misadventure. Invariably, friends or relatives would alert the police about a missing loved one or a friend known to have been swimming or boating on the river. But the petrified woman didn't fit any existing reports of missing persons.

The first newspaper reports appeared the morning after Charlie Wilson found the body and were perfunctory. But by the weekend, newspapers across the country were giving the mysterious case expanded coverage.

The Barrier Daily reported that police believed the petrified woman had been 'struck with a blunt object, probably a blunt bottle.'

The *Sydney Sun* suggested that the case was reminiscent of the infamous Pyjama Girl mystery of the 1930s in which a badly burned female corpse dressed in pyjamas was found in a country drain. The victim's face had been so severely burned that she was potentially unidentifiable. The Pyjama Girl's body was kept in a formalin bath and displayed at Sydney University for over a decade. The Police finally identified the woman using dental records, then charged her husband with murder.

That weekend, when Adelaide tram conductor Harry Salter read a newspaper report about the mystery woman found floating in the River Murray, a shiver went up his spine. The forty-one-year-old headed down to the Adelaide CIB on Monday morning.

Salter told a detective that the description of the woman in the newspaper seemed to fit that of his mother, Margaret Salter, who lived on a sheep property on the Victorian side of the border with her husband, Russell Bath. Salter said he had last heard from his mother seventeen months earlier, in April 1950, when she had written to say that she would be passing through Adelaide on the way to the Barossa Valley Wine festival. She never arrived.

Around this time, his mother's regular practice of writing to relatives and sending gifts to her grandchildren had also ceased. The detective asked if he had reported her missing. He said he now regretted that he hadn't.

For the next hour, Harry Salter gave the investigators a detailed statement about his mother, her life and her connections. Detectives then escorted him to the Police Morgue to view the body. They warned him that it would be a confronting sight. When the sheet was removed, he gasped and turned away. Indeed, it was the worst thing he had ever seen. He half-turned back, taking short glances out of the corner of his eye.

'I don't know, but it could be my mother,' he said.

Salter told detectives that his mother would have been 59 years of age if she were still alive. The last time he saw her had been in January 1950, when she visited his Adelaide home. Every September, she would send him money to place an *In Memoriam* notice in an Adelaide newspaper for his younger brother, Ted, who had died in 1939, aged only twenty-six. His mother had never recovered from the loss. But after April 1950, no letters or presents for the children arrived, and now for the second year in a row, no money had been received for the In Memoriam notice.

A detective pressed Harry Salter again, "Why didn't you make enquiries?"

He shrugged and said he had his reasons but that they were personal.

Harry Salter departed the Adelaide Police Station in a daze. His statement clearly pointed to the likelihood that the body in the morgue was that of his mother. According to Margaret Ellis, the eldest of his two daughters, Harry Salter was never the same again.

4

SUSPECT

The following morning, at 4 am, homicide detectives Gully and Harper set out on the 120 mile drive from Adelaide, northeast to Renmark. On arrival, they met up with Detective Flint and followed him eastward along an unmade road, which cut through windswept, parched and hungry-looking land where even saltbush struggled for existence. Occasionally, a shimmering blue haze on the horizon offered the promise of respite, but never delivered it.

The border crossing into Victoria was marked by a distinct change in the vegetation running north-south as far as the eye could see. The detectives had entered the vast sheep property called Lindsay Point Station. At the main gate, they met with Victorian detective John Killeen who'd driven across from Mildura. Together, they proceeded on a track that led to Lindsay Creek, a tributary of the River Murray.

Lindsay Point Station

Passing a magnificent stand of poplars, a dam fringed by willows, and paddocks with flocks of merino sheep, the detectives' vehicles pulled up at a large timber, tin-roofed homestead.

Station owner Humphrey Kempe heard the sound of a car door closing. When he peered out the window, he was taken aback by the sight of four detectives alighting their vehicles. Kempe, five foot seven, with striking blue eyes and prematurely greying hair, pulled up his braces, put on his wide-brimmed hat and stepped out onto the verandah. He recognised Detective David Flint from his visits to Renmark and gave him a questioning nod. Flint's expression implied that something serious had happened.

Flint introduced his colleagues and explained they were enquiring about a Mrs Bath - formerly Mrs Margaret Salter - who lived at the property.

"Marg?" queried Kempe. "She left here some time back - around April 1950."

Kempe invited them inside his home, but Flint declined the offer.

"Roughly seventeen months ago?" Killeen queried.

"We were overseas at the time. On our return, we learned from Russell - that's Russell Bath - that Marg had gone to live in Melbourne. What's happened?"

Flint got to the point, "We recovered a body from the Murray this week. We believe it may be that of Mrs Bath."

Kempe shook his head in disbelief, "I heard she's been seen around since she left here."

"We need to discuss that with Russell Bath. Is he still working here?"

Kempe nodded and escorted the detectives 150 yards from his homestead to a modest two-bedroom cottage situated on a high bank of Lindsay Creek.

Kempe knocked on the frame of the timber screen door. A shortish, sharp-featured, unshaven man in work clothes appeared from the kitchen.

"Russell, these gentlemen are from the police," said Kempe gravely. "They want to have a word with you."

Bath cocked a sheepish eye at Kempe, then at the detectives standing behind him.

He opened the screen door and ushered them inside.

Kempe returned to the homestead, stunned to think that his longest-serving and most trusted farmhand was caught up in a police investigation.

"What's this about?"asked Bath.

"We are making inquiries," Harper said, "Inquiries concerning the body of a woman found floating in the Murray upstream from Renmark last Wednesday."

Detective Gully motioned for Bath to sit down at the kitchen table. His colleague Harper took a pencil and a small notebook from his coat pocket.

"We have reason to believe it is the body of your wife Margaret, or Marg, as she was known. We have come to find out exactly what happened."

Bath was immediately defensive. He said that Marg was not his wife but his housekeeper. They had never married, but had lived as man and wife.

"Then how long have you been living together?"

"About eleven or twelve years, I should say. She decided to come and look after me, but then we decided to break it up. I told everybody what had happened, as far as my story is concerned."

"And now you will tell us what happened."

Bath said that they had arranged a holiday, after which she was going to take a break of three months and then probably come back. They left Lindsay Point on April 14, 1950, at 5 am to drive to Adelaide to visit her family. They then planned to go to the Vintage Wine Festival in the Barossa Valley.

"Why did you leave so early?" probed Gully.

"We always leave early to get right through to Adelaide."

"Did anybody know that you were leaving so early?"

"The Breens knew we were leaving at 5 am."

"We drove via Renmark. At the railway station, she said to stop the car. She got out and into a 1940 Chevrolet black sedan, which drove off. She said she was going to Victoria. That was the last I ever saw of her."

"Just exactly where in Renmark did you pull up?"

"It was between the railway station gates and Moray Park sheds."

"Which way was the other car travelling?"

"From Renmark."

The Adelaide detectives had heard a similar version from Marg's son, Harry Salter. Bath had turned up in Adelaide a week after she allegedly left him at Renmark Railway Station and called on Harry to see if he'd heard from her.

Detective Gully asked Bath if Marg had given him anything as she got out of the car. He said she had given him nothing.

Gully asked him to have a good think about his answers.

"I'll ask again. Did Margaret hand you anything?"

"She did not."

"Are you absolutely positive?"

"Yes, I am."

"You gave her a large sum of money in an envelope that morning."

"I never gave her money."

"She gave you her engagement ring."

"She did not."

"Are you sure she never gave you her engagement ring in an envelope when she said she was leaving?"

"She did not."

"We interviewed her son, and he tells us that you distinctly told him those things happened."

"He could be telling lies."

"But we are sure that he is not telling lies. He says that you told him that this is how it happened. She handed you her ring in an envelope, and you handed her £100 in an envelope before she disappeared in this other car."

"He might be making a mistake."

"A man couldn't make a mistake about something like that."

"I never gave her any money, and she never gave me any rings."

Harper said firmly, "I would like to hear from your own lips the true story about what happened."

"Well, that's my story, and it's true. Anyway, Marg has been seen since she left me."

Gully interjected, "Who saw her?"

"Mrs Bill Price of Mildura. Alice is her name. She saw her in Stawell since."

Stawell was 220 miles[2] south of Mildura, the closest large town to Lindsay Point.

"How do you know that?"

"My mother saw Alice in Mildura, and Alice told her that she had seen Marg in Stawell. She went into a shop to get some medicine for her child and saw Marg serving behind the counter."

"When did you hear about this?"

"Last Christmas—when she came back from seeing Alice."

"Last Christmas…?" queried Harper. "Did this Alice Price speak to Margaret in Stawell?"

---

[2] 354 kilometers

"I don't know, but she saw Marg there."

"Mrs Price was friendly with Marg, was she?"

"Yes."

"Then you would expect her to speak to her."

"I don't know if Alice spoke to Marg or not. She told my mother that she had seen Marg in Stawell in a shop. She has been seen by several people since she left me."

Detective Gully said, "Well, let's get right back to the start and tell us where you met your wife and how she came to leave you."

While his Adelaide colleagues questioned Bath, Detective David Flint searched the cottage. In cupboards and drawers, he found dozens of items of women's clothing and underwear, some of which appeared to have been newly purchased. He also found a box containing a wedding ring and an engagement ring. He then returned to the kitchen and quietly conferred with Detective Gully, who then returned to the subject of Margaret's rings.

"Did she or did she not hand a wedding ring to you that morning at Renmark?"

"Well, yes, she did."

"Where is the ring now, then?"

"It's in a box inside."

"And she handed you an engagement ring also that morning?"

"Yes."

"Where is that now?"

"With the wedding ring."

"Where did Margaret give you these rings?"

"At Renmark railway station."

"Not long ago, you told me distinctly that she never gave you any rings."

"I never said that."

Bath's story had more twists than a hangman's noose.

Detective Harper reminded Bath that he was taking short-hand.

"Why did you tell lies about that?" pressed Gully.

"It was a mistake I made."

A mistake, indeed.

Bath claimed that he'd given Marg the wedding ring. Later, he admitted that he had not purchased the wedding ring or any other rings.

"Don't you think it strange for a woman to hand you rings that you had never given her in the first place?"

"She handed me them both in an envelope."

"Who bought the rings in the first place?"

"She did."

"If she bought the two rings, why should she hand them back to you?"

"I don't know."

"What did you say when she handed you the rings?'

"It was just too much for me when she said she might not come back."

"She said those words?"

"Yes."

"Let me see her rings now."

The detectives accompanied Bath into the bedroom, where he retrieved a box marked Dean Jewellers - Adelaide.

"These are the rings she handed me."

Bath then indicated a large quantity of women's new and used underclothing, dresses, and two dressing gowns.

Gully quipped, "To me, it seems strange for a woman who apparently has made plans to leave you, not to take all this clothing away with her."

"It does seem as though it was prearranged, doesn't it?"

"Yes. When you say that this mysterious black car came along like it did. Didn't you try and get the number of the car?"

"No. It was dark."

"Couldn't you see what the other driver looked like?" Harper asked.

"No."

"Didn't you try and find out some particulars of where they were going and who she was going with?"

"No."

"You made no effort although you wanted her to stop with you?"

"I wanted her to stop with me."

"You made no effort at all that morning at the Renmark railway station to find out about this other man?"

"No. I didn't get out of the car."

Bath claimed that Marg had packed two cases of clothes and one hat box. In his search of the cottage, Detective Flint found travelling cases full of clothing in the bedroom. He appeared in the doorway.

"Did you help to get her cases out?" he asked.

"No."

"What about the hat box?"

"She didn't take that. It's there now on the wardrobe."

Flint nodded to his colleagues to bring Bath into the bedroom.

"Is that the hat box on the wardrobe?"

"Yes."

Flint took down the hatbox, placed it on the bed, and opened it. In the box were five women's hats and one man's hat.

"Margaret never bothered to take her hats either?" Harper asked.

"No. I brought the hat box back with me."

Gully picked up one of the hats and twirled it a little. Bath clenched a fist tightly and deliberately rubbed his stubbled chin.

Flint piped in with an afterthought, "Did Marg have false teeth?"

"Yes."

"On both upper and lower?"

"Yes"

"Did she used to keep them in night and day?"

"Yes."

"She had no teeth at all?"

"That's right, she had no teeth."

During his search of the bedroom, Flint also found handbags and two pairs of prescription glasses. Bath admitted that she required glasses but couldn't explain why she would leave without them.

Flint motioned to Harper to follow him onto the enclosed verandah. He pointed to what appeared to be a patch of dried blood on the linoleum floor.

Bath claimed that blood had seeped from an old refrigerator but said they were welcome to take the linoleum away with them.

Harper smiled, "We might just do that."

Throughout the interview, Bath repeatedly tripped over his own responses. It was cringe-worthy, like watching a child snared by his own fibbing. But this wasn't about a missing biscuit - this was an investigation into the possible homicide of his de facto wife.

Detective Gully made it clear to Bath that he didn't believe him, that the disappearance of Marg was suspicious, and that Bath had done nothing but implicate himself.

"It all points to me at the moment," Bath admitted, "I can see why I am in it. Anyway, I did stop here, didn't I? It would have been against me if I hadn't, and if I had run away, it would have looked bad."

"Is there anything to run away for?"

"No, not really."

"It looks to me that you have tried to prevent Margaret from leaving you, and when she said she was going forever, you hit her over the head and disposed of her body."

"You are on the wrong road."

"I believe that the woman in the river is Margaret. Is there anything you want to say about how she disappeared?"

"No, I'll let her ride."[3]

While searching the house, Flint discovered a Smith & Wesson pistol. He asked Bath for the registration papers. Bath replied that the gun wasn't registered. There was no suggestion that Bath had shot Margaret, but the unregistered firearm gave detectives grounds to arrest Bath and prevent him from destroying evidence. Victorian detective John Killeen handcuffed Bath, bundled him into his car, and drove from Lindsay Point to Mildura.

Detective Flint stayed at the property, where he took possession of a large quantity of women's clothing, the diamond wedding ring and engagement ring. He then cut out two sections of stained linoleum flooring and bagged them.

At Mildura Police Station, Killeen charged Russell Rufus Bath with possession of an unregistered pistol and placed him in a cell until a magistrate could hear the case.

> **Mystery of River; Arrest**
>
> Mildura. — Detectives investigating the finding of a woman's body floating in the Murray River last Thursday have arrested a station hand and have charged him with the possession of an unregistered pistol.
>
> He is Russell Rufus Bath (42), of Lindsay's Point Station, 40 miles from Mildura.

---

[3] "I've nothing to say on the matter."

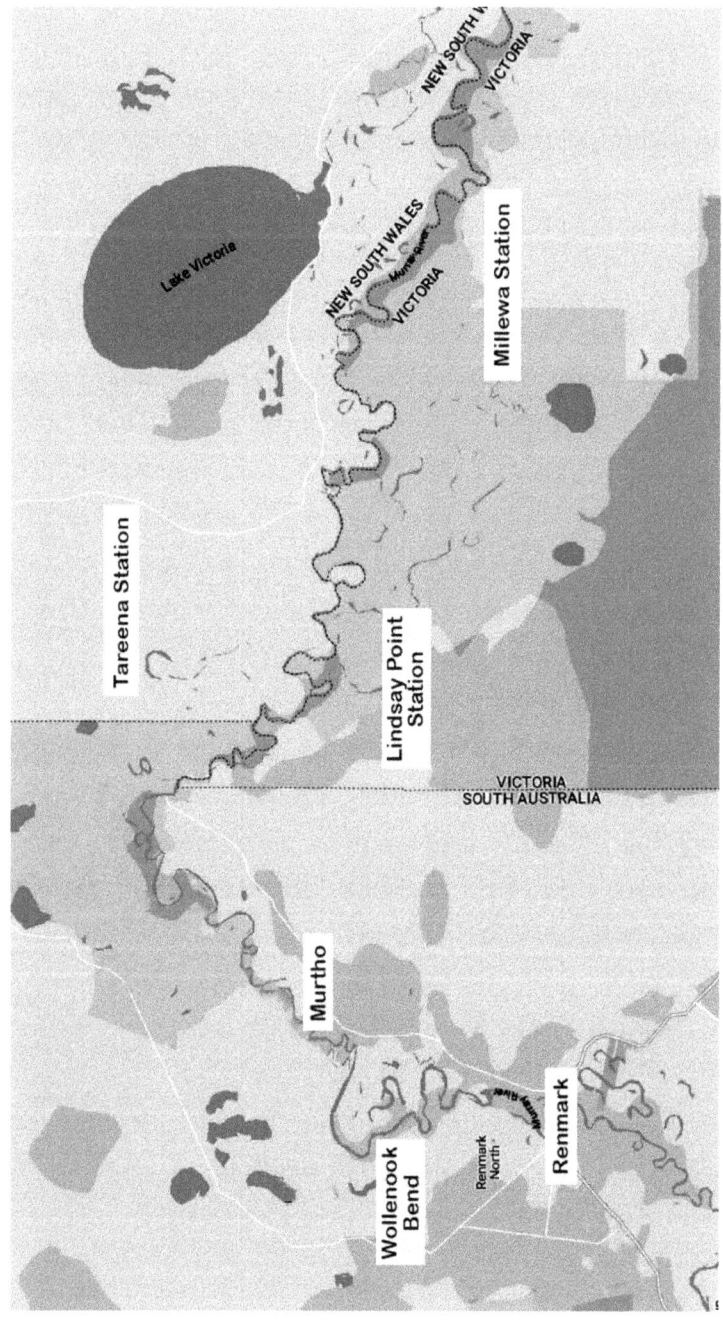

5

HOUSEKEEPER

Margaret Salter came into the world in 1892, the ninth of ten children born to Thomas and Catherine Wright. The Wrights immigrated to South Australia on assisted passage from County Clare, Ireland, in 1879 and settled in North Adelaide.

In 1909, Margaret fell out with her family when she announced that she had fallen pregnant to a local lad, Henry Salter. They were both only seventeen. Three days after the birth of their son, Henry George (Harry), they married at the home of their midwife, Emily Senn, who was the only witness to the nuptials.

Henry worked on the Adelaide trams. Three more children, Mary, Ted, and Timothy, arrived in quick succession, but Mary and Timothy died as infants.

On leaving school, Henry and Margaret's eldest son, Harry, trained as a cobbler. He also embraced traditionalist Catholicism, and with it, a stern, granite-like immovability on issues of morality. At that time, Catholic priests railed against divorce and birth control, preached about the sanctity of the family and encouraged their male followers to be good sons, husbands and fathers. Therefore, it came as a shock when young Harry eventually discovered that he had been born out of wedlock. His response was to flee the family home in disgust. His distressed mother, Margaret, went to the police and filed a missing persons report.

> Youth Missing: Since he left his home in Capper Street, Kent Town, at 7.45 o'clock yesterday morning to go to work, Henry George Salter, aged 18 years, has not been seen by his mother, Mrs Margaret. Salter. She is anxious to hear anything of his whereabouts. It has been ascertained that the missing youth did not reach his place of employment. He is described as being 5 ft. 4 in. in height, of stout build, with a fresh complexion, dark hair, and brown eyes. He is a boot repairer, wearing a navy blue suit, green-coloured felt hat, black shoes and tan socks when last seen.

Harry eventually returned home, but worse was to come. The following year, he learned to his horror that his mother had filed for divorce from his father. Margaret had discovered that Henry had taken a mistress - Miss Ettie Freer.

In court, Henry denied the allegations and counterclaimed that Margaret was guilty of misconduct with a man whose name he did not know. The court found for the petitioner Margaret Salter and granted a decree nisi.

The affair and subsequent divorce were plastered across the newspapers. Then, to young Harry's further embarrassment, his father married Ettie Freer.[4]

For Margaret, these events marked the beginning of a decade of trauma. Her mother, father and a sister passed away. In 1935, she was seriously injured in a car accident and spent weeks convalescing.

In 1936, Harry refused to attend his brother Ted's wedding because it was to be held in an Anglican Church.

Three years later, in April 1939, when young Harry married Patricia Eveline Myers, Margaret suffered the indignity of attending the marriage ceremony along with her former husband and his new wife, Ettie.

Five months after Harry's wedding, Ted unexpectedly died. He'd suffered a brain haemorrhage at the age twenty-six, and left a wife and baby son. Harry maintained his dogged religious stance and refused to attend his brother's Protestant funeral.

In 1940, Harry sent his mother to Renmark, one hundred and fifty miles away, to help her gain some distance from her grief-ridden past.

At the age of forty-eight, Margaret suddenly had to adapt to a self-sufficient life in a small town. She applied for a position as a laundress at the local hospital. The matron saw

---

[4] In 1945, Harry Salter Snr divorced Ettie, a resident of Northfield Mental Hospital on the grounds of mental defect without the likelihood of recovery.

in Margaret a sturdy, tidy and reliable woman with a lifetime of experience carrying out domestic duties. The role was hot and heavy work, manipulating heavy bedlinen in and out of vast boilers, then manhandling them through wringers and hanging them end-to-end on lines.

It was at the Renmark Hospital that she met Russell Bath. He was a labourer, sixteen years her junior, and extremely reserved. At the time, he was boarding with his parents in their small, overcrowded cottage on Sixteenth Street, Renmark.

Bath told Margaret he'd taken a job with Humphrey Kempe on his sheep property across the Victorian border, at Lindsay Point. He asked her to come with him as his housekeeper, and if it worked out, he would marry her.

In the early 1940s, the journey from Renmark to Lindsay Point Station felt more like a hundred miles than thirty. It wasn't merely the poor condition of the unmade road, with its potholes and numerous bone-jarring corrugated stretches. It was also the fact that every few miles, a gate blocked their way. There were thirteen gates in all, and they had to stop, get out, open the gate, drive the car through and close it - thirteen times. First-time travellers would invariably ponder the purpose of the gates as nary an animal could be seen, other than the occasional scurrying rabbit or kangaroo at dusk. Sand drifts were also a nightmare. In the summer heat, with temperatures often reaching 120 degrees[5], travellers could die if they found themselves bogged. If ever there was a stretch of worthless land on the Australian continent worthy of the moniker 'the Devil's anvil', this was it.

Twenty-five miles into the journey, at the state border, they entered Lindsay Point Station.

Two years earlier, First World War veteran Humphrey Kempe, sold up his neighbouring property, Millewa, and purchased what he acknowledged was considered wasteland.

In his book, *The Astonished Earth*, Kemp wrote:

> In 1939 Lindsay Point had no name. It was simply a section of Murray River frontage country marked on an old Land and Survey Department plan as Old George's Paddock. A dusty place — windswept, unsheltered, eroded and bare, a stage where sun and mirage danced together on the plain and heat lay heavy on the low hills above. Almost as we left a comfortable, established homestead to move in and commence our work in 1939, the War began and, with it, our own war effort. Building materials, fencing wire and machinery, essential hardware and stores were soon hard to find on or off the market.

Using whatever resources he could muster, Kempe had begun experimenting with irrigation practices he'd

---
[5] Forty-eight degrees Celsius

witnessed in the Middle East during the First World War. Lindsay Point had one great advantage. It sat on a tributary of the mighty River Murray. Twenty feet deep and two hundred feet across, Lindsay Creek was, by any measure, a substantial waterway and provided him the opportunity to irrigate tens of thousands of acres.

To realise his dream, Kempe required substantial manpower, but with Australia at war again, labour was scarce, and even men in need of work baulked at living and toiling on such harsh country. The surroundings were so uninviting that a friend of Kempe's described it in a moment of candour as "a damned and dusty hole." But Kempe contrived a clever strategy to recruit residential labour. On his visits to Renmark to pick up provisions, he would call by the Police Station to see who was in the cells - not out of curiosity - but to find able-bodied men who needed a break in life; men willing to work and learn skills that would hopefully keep them on the right side of the law.

> On one occasion, being short of men and labour hard to get, I called at the distant Police Station with the intention of getting a reasonably reliable man whom the police might think would be all the better for a spell out of town. It was all pleasantly informal. After discussing the question of a workman, the Sergeant, agreeing that he might be able to help, said, "There's no one in the cells just now, but I let one out this morning who might be useful. Let's go down to the pub." Sure enough, Jack was there and likely to get

himself into trouble again. The Sergeant took him by the arm, then up the street to the cells, saying, "When you want your man, you can have him, today or tomorrow. He will be safe there until you are ready to leave town." A little unconventional but very convenient.[6]

One such recruit was Russell Rufus Bath, who was to become Kempe's most loyal employee.

---

[6] Humphrey Kempe, *The Astonished Earth*

6

WONDERLAND

In 1941, Margaret wrote to her son Harry in Adelaide, saying that she had married Russell Bath and that they were now living together on Lindsay Point Station. The marriage, in fact, had not occurred, but Margaret knew better than to wage war with her staunchly Catholic son.

Kempe had allocated the couple a small cottage perched on the high bank of Lindsay Creek.

Kempe's daughter, Merridy,[7] a teenager at the time, recalled that Marg, or Mrs Bath as she was always called, was pleasant but quiet and self-contained. Each morning she came to the Kempe homestead for two hours to clean and do the washing. Merridy remembered her as a short, large-framed woman who did her chores well, but who, despite her many years of service, never became close to the Kempe family.

---

[7] Interviewed by the author when she was ninety-six years of age, in 2019.

Following her duties at the homestead, Marg cooked, washed and cleaned the cottage she shared with Russell. All employees benefited from free meat, milk, fruit and vegetables grown on the property. Every six weeks or so, a paddle steamer would call by Lindsay Point stocked with just about everything imaginable, from brooms to radios, cosmetics to sewing machine oil.

Marg was universally liked by families along the river. She and Russell often spent their weekends and even holidays on neighbouring properties.

For Russell Bath, work was hard physical toil from sun-up to sunset. Kempe admired him for his ability with machinery and his tireless work installing and experimenting with irrigation equipment. Even through the drought of 1943-45, Lindsay Point boasted sixteen head of sheep to the acre - a yield unheard of in such harsh country.

Word travelled far and wide about Lindsay Point. Agriculturalists, scientists and even Ministers of the Crown were keen to behold the potential of irrigation. In January 1945, two buses conveyed George Jenkins, the Victorian Government Minister for Agriculture, and his party to Lindsay Point to see Kempe's miracle. Beyond Renmark, the buses became bogged in sand. All hands, including the Minister's, were applied to return the vehicles onto solid ground.

As the border approached, the official travellers noted the shimmer on the plain change from a yellow hue to a dusty blue-green. Past the border post into Victoria, the land was impressively thick with clover produced not only by the application of water to the arid land but also by years of scientific experimentation with different varieties of grasses and legumes. That day, Russell and Marg were called upon to host the important visitors.

The *Murray Pioneer* reported:

> The trip was arranged by the Renmark Corporation, which is advocating the development of the River flats for pasture growing as a post-war undertaking. In the absence of Mr Kempe, the party was shown over the property by Mr Russell Bath. The Minister appeared to be well impressed with the possibilities of growing pastures under irrigation.

At Christmas, Russell was accustomed to driving Marg down to Adelaide to visit her son, Harry and his family. By this time, Harry and Patricia had two girls, Patricia - known by her middle name of Margaret, and Helen. Marg was particularly interested in her two granddaughters. When young Margaret was old enough, Russell and Marg began taking her back to Lindsay Point for the remainder of the school holidays.

> They came down, picked me up in the old Packard, and took me up there. It was a big place - at least, it seemed big as a small child. It was a nice house made of timber - timber verandah, timber floors, and linoleum on the floors. It had two bedrooms, a kitchen and a lounge. It had a tin roof, and when it rained, well, I liked the sound. Of course, in those days, there was no TV. We used to sit outside on the verandah after dinner and listen to the radio. I'd ride the horse and used to go sit in the sheds and watch

them shearing the sheep and sometime even watch them slaughter a sheep. I thought that was something out of this world. Living in the city, you don't see anything like that.⁸

Indeed, for a child, Lindsay Point was a wonderland. The pastures were feeding grounds for kangaroos, emus, quail, magpies, parrots, galahs, herons, wood ducks and black ducks. Occasionally, a squadron of pelicans would fly overhead in formation.⁹

In young Margaret's eyes, 'Grandma Bath' was bubbly and sentimental. Without fail, she would post gifts for her and her sister's birthdays and at Christmas. She also recalled that her grandmother would send money in the post every

---

⁸ Margaret Ellis interviewed by the author
⁹ *The Astonished Earth*, by Humphrey Kemp

September to her father, Harry, to place an *In Memoriam* notice in the *Adelaide Advertiser* for his brother, Ted. She also remembered that Ted's sudden death in 1939 at the age of twenty-six had left her grandmother permanently heartbroken, and that she often wore black as a sign of her ongoing grief.

In his statement to police, Harry Salter said that the last time he saw his mother, she had hinted that all was not well in her relationship with Russell Bath.

> In January 1950, when she came to Adelaide, she said, "I will go silly if I have to go up to the property further up the Murray as Russell has been asked to do. I don't want to go. I want him to come to Adelaide and get a job, but he won't."

In his statement, Harry Salter also recalled in detail the visit from Russell Bath at Easter 1950, a week after his mother allegedly left Bath at the Renmark Railway Station.

> Easter Sunday was 24th April. On that day, Russell Bath came to my home. I met him in the side drive. I said, "Where is Mum?" He said, "She has gone to Melbourne for a holiday." He came inside as we had visitors. Later on the same day, he said, "Where is Mum? I thought she might have been here." I said, "What happened?" He said, "We were going down to

the Barossa Valley Festival. When we got to Renmark, she got out of the car and said, 'That is as far as I am going.' She then got into a black car." I said, "Did you get the number of it?" Bath said, "No, They just drove off." I said, "I think I would have tried to get some information, Russell."

Bath had an old Packard motorcar, and I presumed they were on their own at this stage. My mother was known as 'Marg Bath' at Lindsay Point. I knew that a relation of mine, John Breen[10] and his wife, were living on Lindsay Point Station when my mother and Russell were supposed to have left Renmark to go to the Barossa Valley Festival. The Breens told me that mum and Russell left on 14th April 1950. I also heard they intended to stop at Mr Obst's place in the Barossa Valley. I have heard nothing of (my mother) Margaret Salter, nor received any letters from her since March 1950, and from what I can understand, nor has anybody else.

Harry Salter also told detectives that Russell Bath turned up at his home on the Tuesday after Easter 1951, eleven months after she allegedly left him at Renmark Railway Station. Salter recalled the conversation as such:

"Have you sighted anything of Marg?" Bath asked.

"No, have you?" I said.

---

[10] John Joseph Breen was the great nephew of Margaret Salter. He was the grandson of Margaret's sister Bridget Florence Wright. He resided at Lindsay Point with his wife Joyce and 2 year old daughter, Melvina.

"Some people tell me they have seen her in Melbourne."

"Who are they?" I asked.

"I can't tell you now. Anyway, somebody else saw Marg at the Adelaide Railway Station."

"Who is that?"

"I can't tell you now."

"I have heard nothing."

Bath said, "What will I do with her clothes, as the Boss wants the house for another married couple. I have to go into the single men's quarters, and her clothes are in the wardrobe."

I said, "If she has left, she is not going to come back, so the best thing to do is sell them."

He didn't answer.

I said, "Have you notified the Police?"

"No, if she wants to come back, the door is still open to her."

According to Margaret's granddaughter, Margaret Ellis, her father was taken aback when he finally learnt that his mother was not married to Russell Bath.

It came as a big surprise to my father when he found out his mother hadn't married Russell Bath. He was a strict Catholic. In those days, you never heard of people living together if they weren't married. I always knew her as Grandma Bath. When you're a kid and have two people living together, you'd think they'd be married.

Margaret Ellis was ten-years-old when she learned of the body recovered from the River Murray and how the Police had linked it to Grandma Bath's disappearance.

> My father told me that he hadn't heard from my grandmother. He said, "I don't know what's happening." He knew how much I loved her. And being the oldest, he confided in me. He said that he'd been to the Police Station and that they wanted me to give them a statement. So he took me up to the Adelaide Police Station to tell them what I knew.

The police asked Margaret about her last visit to Lindsay Point.

> I told them they had an argument the last time I was there - and it was a strong one. But I couldn't remember what it was about. I remember Russell was always reluctant to come down and pick me up, but I think she told him to. He used to have a drink or two when I was there, but I never saw him being violent. Maybe he was on his best behaviour.

7

WRATH

The morning after his arrest for possession of the unlicensed gun, the duty sergeant delivered Bath to the local courthouse. That afternoon, a front-page story in Adelaide's *The News* linked Bath's arrest to the case of the woman found in the River Murray:

> Mildura, Wed: A station hand arrested late yesterday by police investigating the "body in the river" case, appeared in Mildura Police Court today charged with having been in possession of an unregistered pistol. The man, Russell Rufus Bath, 42, of Lindsay Point Station, was remanded to appear at Merbein (Victoria) Police Court on October 18. He was allowed bail of £100. Bath was arrested near the South Australia-Victoria border yesterday by Detective Inspector Gully and Detective Harper, of Adelaide; Detective Flint, of Renmark and Detective Killeen of

Mildura. The police visited the station to investigate the disappearance of Mrs Margorie (sic) Salter, a housekeeper. Today, they are still at the station interviewing employees in an effort to establish whether the calcified body of a woman found in the River Murray at Renmark last Wednesday is that of Mrs Salter. They are working on the assumption that the missing woman was murdered, her body buried in a shallow grave, and washed out by floodwaters.

After his release on bail, Bath immediately felt the wrath of locals. They had read the newspaper stories about the body found in the River Murray, and believed they had a murderer in their midst. At best, Bath experienced the cold shoulder; at worst, he was verbally and physically abused.

Whenever confronted, Bath insisted that he had played no part in Margaret's disappearance and claimed that it was all as much a shock to him as to everyone else. But for all his protestations of innocence, he showed little outward emotion and certainly expressed no concern that the body found in the river might be that of his de facto wife.

Lindsay Point Station owner Humphrey Kempe had great regard for Russell Bath's work and was shocked at the thought that he may have killed Marg. She had, after all, been the homestead's housekeeper for over a decade. In his memoir, The Astonished Earth, Kempe didn't mention the case specifically but did write that isolation and alcohol often proved a combustible mix at Lindsay Point Station.

The men on the place, the regular orchard hands and station hands, were reliable, good people and our children, when young, made great friends with these men who were always kind and helpful to them. Naturally, a few wild men and drinkers would occasionally be among those engaged, but they did not last long nor cause much trouble. There were one or two traumatic cases. One went a little silly with a knife, another with a gun, and so on, but largely these were fairly decent types who found their oppressions and repressions rising to the surface when removed from a closely settled environment to a lonely one.

As the prime suspect in a homicide investigation, Bath expected that his tenure at Lindsay Point would be at an end. Following his release on bail, he returned to his cottage, packed a suitcase and prepared to depart the property for good. But Humphrey Kempe came by and said that he had discussed the matter with his wife, Louise, and they agreed that until found otherwise, he was innocent of any wrongdoing and welcome to stay. In reality, Kempe was fulfilling a promise to detectives that he'd do what he could to prevent their suspect from fleeing.

For Russell Rufus Bath, the days ahead were likely occupied with one thought - how to convince the world of his innocence. The alternative was the hangman's noose.

I JUST SHOT THE MISSUS

Under South Australian law, a person found guilty of murder would be sentenced to death by hanging. Indeed, such a sentence was mandatory.

Twenty years earlier, Thomas Blyth, a work colleague of Margaret's former father-in-law, Henry Salter, was found guilty of murder. The 39-year-old former tram conductor had indulged in a six-month drinking bout and began terrorising his wife over an alleged affair she'd had with another man named Warren. When Blyth's temper turned to violence, Mrs Blyth left home with their two daughters. Blyth then purchased a pistol, tracked down his wife and shot her point blank. Following the incident, Blyth turned up at his local watering hole and told the publican, "I just shot the missus."

Blyth was convicted of murder and hanged in Adelaide Goal in January 1930. Just before the hood was placed over his head, he quipped,

"There is only one thing I regret, and that is that I did not get Warren."

In the 1950s, every Australian state except Queensland practised capital punishment, though with varying degrees of enthusiasm. If Russell Bath were to be tried and found guilty in South Australia, there was every chance he would be executed, whereas if charged in the State of Victoria, he would have a better chance of beating death. Over the previous dozen years, only four of the two hundred and four people convicted of murder in Victoria had actually been hanged.

Each time Bath opened his mouth, he seemed to implicate himself in Margaret's disappearance. However, to charge him with her murder, the investigators still needed to make a definitive identification of the petrified woman.

9

THIS STRANGEST OF CRIMES

The story of *The Petrified Woman* featured in radio news bulletins and newspapers and quickly became a media sensation across Australia. On Saturday, 6 October, Adelaide's *The Mail* newspaper encapsulated the state of play ten days into the investigation.

FREAK OF NATURE IN BODY MYSTERY

Has one of Nature's strongest freaks — the turning of a woman's body into stone — combined with a River Murray flood to expose the closely held secret of a brutal murder? This is the question facing detectives in an attempt to unravel the mystery surrounding last week's discovery of a stone-like, featureless body of a woman floating in the flooded River Murray near Renmark. If the victim were murdered, fate has thwarted a murderer's attempt to dispose of the victim and conceal the crime forever. For instead of Nature following its normal process of decomposing a body, a phenomenon caused by the action over a long period of limestone on the body had begun to turn the flesh into stone. And had the river not flooded and cast up its ghastly secret last week, the transformation may have continued until the body was a pillar of stone. Such oddities have occurred in limestone caves in other parts of the world. Limestone cliffs, caves, and calciferous soil are common along stretches of the winding Murray. It was this fact, coupled with a report of the disappearance of a station housekeeper in the district, that sent detectives this week to the flooded river on the SA-Vic. border. Plump, jovial Mrs Margaret Salter, 59, who had been widely known and respected in the district for many years, disappeared from Lindsay Point Station 17 months ago. She was divorced before 1941 and, after working as a laundress at Renmark Hospital, joined the staff at the station's spacious homestead a few miles inside the Victorian border. She regularly wrote to her son and daughter-in-law in Adelaide and took a proud interest in her grandchildren. In April last year, her letters ceased. The children's birthdays passed unnoticed by her. A report went the rounds that she had gone on a holiday to the Barossa Valley Vintage Festival. Station hands couldn't explain why she did not return. She had seemed contented enough with life at the homestead.

Her disappearance was never reported to the Police. But neither is the disappearance of many others who vanish each year. But after a local fisherman found the body floating 12 miles upstream from Renmark in the swirling current at Woolenook Bend, Adelaide tram conductor Mr Harry Salter thought it might be that of his long-lost mother. The possibility seemed more feasible when it was found that Lindsay Point Station, where she worked, had a shallow arm of the Murray running almost up to the back door of the homestead. There is some limestone between the homestead and the spot where the body was found. Police also found that although Mrs Salter had reportedly left on holiday, she had left behind some new dresses and her rings and jewellery. Mrs Salter's description resembled at least the height and stoutness of the body.

Scouting vast swamp areas along the river's course this week, Detective Inspector Gully and Detective Harper of Adelaide, Detective Flint of Renmark, and Detective Killeen, of Mildura (Vic.) worked their way across the border in search of a cave or grave from which floodwater might have delivered the body. They returned with soil samples and other possible clues for analysis by Adelaide scientists.

This weekend Police would still not express an opinion on whether the body was that of the missing housekeeper. If this strangest of crimes is to be solved, they face the tough assignment of identifying a body almost devoid of vital identification features. The hands which might have yielded fingerprints were missing. There were no teeth which might have been traced to the records of some dentist. Even the toes and hair, which might have yielded clues, were gone. Would there be a murderer so callous as to rid his victim of fingers to prevent identification? Or was there another answer? The victim's skull had been badly fractured. Did this cause her death, or was she knocked unconscious and killed by other means? What was the motive for murder? What was the significance of the diamond-shaped marks found on the right leg? If they were caused by the body being carried on a wire mattress, will the river at some future date give up this clue as it did the body? Some of the answers may already be known to the Police.

With investigations uncompleted, their findings must remain secret. One fact emerges. Newspapers and radio stations throughout every State in the Commonwealth have published stories this week of the missing housekeeper, but Mrs Margaret Salter is still missing.

The mention of the diamond-shaped marks found on the Petrified Woman's leg prompted Adelaide resident Mrs Eva Edge to contact the police. She said that she'd seen the newspaper report about the body found in the river and had information that she believed could identify the body. Mrs Edge said that Margaret Salter had been involved in a motor lorry accident in the 1930s, and her leg had been badly torn by barbed wire. She said that Margaret didn't want to go to a hospital, so she had dressed the wounds and nursed Mrs Salter at her home. Mrs Edge told the police that she believed she could identify the scars the pathologist found on the right thigh of the corpse. Moreover, she had photographs of the wounded leg.

The police, however, turned down Mrs Edge's offer to view the body, unconvinced that identification by this method alone would be enough to sway the Coroner.

> Mrs. Eva Alice Edge
> 14 Charles Rd.
> Plympton
>
> 1935. Deceased in an accident on Old Hutt Rd. and had one of he legs badly torn by barbed wot wire. Then lived at 7 Grange Lane Norwood.
>
> Claiming I las Pictures at that time.

10

WITNESSES

For the joint team of detectives from South Australia, Victoria and New South Wales, the most pressing line of inquiry now centred on witnesses whom Russell Bath claimed had seen Margaret alive after the date they believed she had been murdered. The investigators suspected that Bath was feeding people with false sightings to remove suspicion from himself.

New South Wales detectives interviewed Mr George Coombs, who worked on a station on the New South Wales side of the River Murray. He recalled Bath telling him that Margaret was in Western Australia.

The New South Wales Police also interviewed Valda Jones, who worked at Romano's Hotel in Wagga Wagga. Miss Jones said that in April 1951, a full year after Marg's sudden departure, she and a girlfriend had been working at the Victor Hotel at Victor Harbour in South Australia. One day, she saw a person whom she recognised as Margaret Bath.

"It was my day off from work," she said, "I was down the street in the morning and saw a man and a woman in the main street. They came around the corner and were walking away from me when I saw the woman, and I thought it was my aunt Margaret. But I was only going by her build."

"How far were you from her?"

"About fifty yards, I'd say."

Valda claimed she saw the couple again later that day.

"That afternoon, I was on the beach when I saw the man and woman I'd seen that morning. They would have been about 30 yards from me, but the woman had her back to me most of the time. I again thought it was my aunt."

"Did you speak to her?"

"I never spoke to the woman, and she at no time recognised me."

"You didn't go up and check to see if it was her and say hello?"

"I didn't approach her as I'd been told by my mother that she had run away with another man."

The detective asked if she had recently been speaking with Russell Bath.

"About nine months ago, I saw Uncle Russell at my mother's place. I had a conversation with him, but he didn't mention his wife."

"You say you saw his wife at Victor Harbour, but you didn't mention that to him?" he said sceptically.

"To the best of my recollection, I never mentioned it."

The detective suspected she was lying.

"Are you certain about any of what you have told me?"

"I could not definitely say that it was my aunt (Marg) that I saw at Victor Harbour. I was only going by her appearance. It was only on the one day that I saw her. Melva Binder was with me when I saw the man and woman, and I think I mentioned it to her."

Detectives then interviewed Valda's girlfriend, Melva Binder, but she had no recollection of either seeing the missing woman or of Valda Jones ever mentioning her.

Victorian detectives visited a modest fibro cottage in Boyden Street, Mildura, to interview Mrs Alice Price. Russell Bath had claimed that Alice told his mother she'd seen Margaret working behind the counter in a shop in the Victorian town of Stawell, more than 220 miles south of Mildura.

Alice's husband, William Price, came to the door but declined to admit the detectives inside and refused to allow them to interview his wife. The Prices then went into hiding.

It transpired that the only two witnesses who alleged to have seen Marg - Alice Price and Valda Jones - were both related to Russell Bath. If the chief suspect in the case thought their testimonies would clear him of suspicion of murder, he was mistaken.

Detective David Flint called at the Renmark residence of fifty-two-year-old fruit grower Donald Bruce. On opening the door, Bruce noticed Flint's shiny black shoes, dark Anthony Squires suit and felt hat, and immediately suspected he was about to be harassed.

The previous year, a Renmark policeman had telephoned the fruit grower about a traffic accident involving his truck. Bruce mistook the caller as a practical joker and told him in no uncertain terms where to go. He also told him to come to his front gate within the half-hour, and he would 'fix' him. Bruce had been genuinely surprised when a policeman on a motorcycle duly arrived within the half-hour to charge him with using obscene language over the phone. When the Renmark Court dismissed the obscene language charge, the police appealed to the High Court. The full bench of the High Court considered the appeal to be a waste of its time and upheld the original decision. Don Bruce suspected that the police would make life difficult for him if they crossed paths again.

Detective Flint sensed that Bruce was still bristling about the incident and assured him this visit had nothing to do with the former matter.

Flint explained that he was inquiring about Russell Bath and his relationship with Margaret Salter and had heard that he was a close friend of the couple.

Bruce said that he'd gone duck shooting at the Lindsay Point property several times. On one occasion, Russell told him that Margaret had gone off after a 'tiff'. Initially, Russell said it was to do with 'her bloody relations.' But the story later flipped when Bath quoted Margaret saying, "This is the last time you will see me. You and your bloody relations can go to buggery."

Don Bruce also recalled Russell Bath saying that Margaret was going through a 'change of life' and suffering from nervous strain. Bath told him about her leaving him at Renmark Railway Station in a black Chevrolet. But he said that Bath told his wife a version of the story in which the colour of the vehicle was cream.

Clearly, Bath couldn't lie straight in bed.

On information supplied by Harry Salter, Adelaide detectives also interviewed Margaret's great nephew, John Breen and his wife, Joyce. When Margaret disappeared, they were living at the Lindsay Point property with their two-year-old daughter, Melvina.

"At this time, I knew that Marg and Russell intended to go on holiday for a fortnight," Breen said, "and I knew they intended to go to the Barossa Valley and Adelaide. They left about April 14, 1950, and must have left early in the morning."

"When did you next see Russell Bath?"

"Russell returned to Lindsay Point about the usual time for him to return from his holiday, but Margaret wasn't with him. I heard that Russell had been seen in Renmark during his holidays. When he returned, I said, 'What happened?' and he said, 'We had started off early, and we got as far as the Railway Station at Renmark, and she leaned over and switched off the ignition and said, "I am leaving you here."

She handed me an envelope with the wedding ring in it. She got her bags out of the back, and I gave her an envelope with £100 in it. She got out into a black car coming past from the direction of Renmark going to Mildura, and she climbed into that with her bags, and away they went.'"

"Did he say what he did after she left him?"

"He said that he had spent a portion of his holidays at Cal Lal or somewhere near there."

Cal Lal was an old settlement across the River Murray from Lindsay Point, near Rufus Creek.

"Did he say anything else about Margaret leaving him?" asked Detective Gully.

"He said, 'I have kept the house open, and I won't sell the furniture in case she does come back.'"

"How well did you know the missing woman?"

"Mrs Salter, or Bath, as she was called up there, is my grandmother's sister."

"Since she disappeared, have you heard from her?"

"No, I haven't seen or heard of her since. That said, I received a letter from Bill Phillips at Tareena Station, and he said they'd heard that Margaret had been seen in Mildura."

The detectives headed to Tareena station, which sat on a salt swamp north of Lindsay Point on the New South Wales side of the River Murray. Half a century back, this had been frontier country. A tribe of thirty Indigenous people, who lived as their ancestors had for tens of thousands of years, defiantly held out against the takeover of their lands by white settlers. But as was prevalent across much of the continent, the sound of the didgeridoo and clapsticks had inevitably gave way to the clamour of the tractor.

William 'Bill' Phillips was a newcomer to the area, having only taken over as manager of Tareena station in the late 1940s. He was shocked by the arrival of a black sedan at his wool shed and the sight of men in suits and ties emerging from the vehicle.

"Can I help you?" Phillips said, wiping his brow.

"We're making enquiries about Russell and Margaret Bath."

"Yes, I know Russell and Marg."

"How well do you know them?"

"I used to board with them at Lindsay Point Station. My wife and I are friends of them both, and they stopped over with us several times."

Phillips described Russell Bath as a retiring type and Marg as very nervous and highly-strung. Even so, he said they seemed very happy together, and she was a good cook and a jolly type. Curiously, Phillips said he felt she was not the type to commit suicide.

"I knew that they were intending to go on holidays," he said, "and it was understood that they would come and stay with us for a short time. In April 1950, Russell arrived at my homestead in his Packard car. He arrived just before lunch or just as we were having lunch. He walked in and appeared upset. He was alone. I thought Margaret was hiding outside, so I went outside to look. She wasn't there. I said, 'Where's Marg?' And he said, 'She hasn't come'. I said, 'Why?' He said, 'She has had a nervous breakdown and has left me.' He told me that she had left him in Renmark. I haven't heard of Mrs Bath from that day to this, although we were very friendly with her."

Wilkinson's Cliffs

Bill Phillips wasn't certain whether Russell Bath arrived on April 14 or the following day. But Bath later confirmed it was the 14th when Margaret allegedly left him.

And therein lay another mystery. The trip to Tareena Station was at most two hours by car. What took place in the other four hours between his and Margaret's arrival at Renmark Railway Station and Russell Bath's arrival at Tareena Station?

The investigators asked Phillips if he knew of any limestone country upstream of Woolenook Bend.

"I know the country and the river around Woolenook Bend, and Russell Bath would also know the country. The only limestone country upriver near Woolenook Bend is around Wilkinson's Cliffs, and the Murtho Road runs close to the cliffs. There are caves in this area, and when the river is in flood, the water would reach these caves. All the cliffs are on the southern side of the river."

Russell Bath was indeed acquainted with this country. He was born in Murtho.

MURTHOITES

Russell Rufus Bath had never ventured very far from the River Murray. Indeed, he came into the world on June 15, 1909, at the riverside settlement of Murtho, twelve and a half miles upstream from Renmark.

Fifteen years before his birth, the South Australian government had established a settlement at Murtho to help the unemployed. They were the early days of what became a severe economic depression, and the powers that be came up with a bold experiment: legislate for associations of twenty or more settlers to hold land and work it as a community. As well as relieving the immediate economic distress, the aim was to educate parents and children in rural life and develop previously unoccupied land, thus bringing idle hands and idle lands together.[11]

---

[11] *Evening Journal* (Adelaide), Friday 15 November 1895, page 3

According to an 1895 edition of the *Evening Journal,* Murtho was established as a quasi-socialist commune, but with a twist.

> Its members must be capitalists— to some extent at least— the minimum payment to join being £40 per head. The other settlers call the Murthoites 'gentlemen villagers.' They are organised under the Village Settlement Act, but they do not seek any Government advance. This settlement is socialistic in its basis, with some of its members having strong affinities with the New Australians.[12] This little band has done wonders in clearing and planting. There are but ten members on the ground as yet, three of whom are accompanied by their wives. They have a small pumping plant erected and have cleared, fenced, and planted about 100 acres, besides the erection of two or three fairly comfortable buildings. Their site stands perhaps 150 ft. above the river, and the soil is as rich as any we have seen. Wheat, potatoes, and trees all look well. Here they have a body, not of the unemployed poor, as in the case of the other villagers, but of respectable and fairly well-to-do citizens, who are dissatisfied with existing social arrangements and are resolved to try to realise true brotherhood in the bush, which they believe to be impossible in the city. I understand that they all share alike, irrespective of the amount they put in, and should any member leave, the

---

[12] New Australia was a Utopian settlement founded by 238 members of the New Australian Movement in Paraguay, South America in 1893

rest are not pledged to refund him anything. They believe that human nature will improve so much under these new and favourable conditions that they may trust one another absolutely. Who does not hope that success may crown so worthy an aim?

Rather than live in rudimentary humpies or tents, the settlers constructed stone houses on the cliff overlooking the River Murray. The typical home had timber-slatted ceilings, a fireplace, and some even boasted wallpaper.

By January 1897, the 'Murthonians' had almost seventy acres under irrigation. But irrigating was expensive, and the cost of transporting provisions and produce by river was dearer per ton than from London to Adelaide.

In 1899, *The Chronicle* reported that most of the settlers had left Murtho. The grand quasi-socialist experiment was dead.

> It failed absolutely. The reasons may thus be summarised — unpractical settlers without experience and the unsuitability of the soil for economic working.

The Chronicle suggested that the land would ultimately be made good if placed in private hands. It was eventually sold off to experienced men, who by 1906 had tens of thousands of acres under wheat.

By 1908, Murtho was attracting large numbers of itinerant workers and their families in search of employment. Some were experienced all-rounders, who settled into the community, but most were seasonal workers. One such family was the Baths. Russell Bath Snr., and his wife, Annie, arrived in 1908 with four young children aged between two and eight, and another on the way.

In May 1909, glorious rains swept across southern Australia. Midwives of the era mused that rain was a good omen for an easy birth. That may have been so, but three weeks later, when Russell Bath was born, the River Murray was rising and threatening to flood. The rains came again in August for three long weeks and gave succour even to those who regarded floods as a bad omen.

In October, the flood finally arrived and delivered a tragedy for the Murtho community. While crossing the river by punt, three men and twenty-one horses were swept away by the river. Six horses and forty-year-old Murtho farmer August Greatz drowned. Greatz had been a well-known figure in the district and respected as one of the best farmers in the surrounding country. His body was found in a lagoon two miles downstream. The tragedy was felt throughout the Murtho community.

Not long afterwards, the Baths packed up their meagre belongings and left Murtho. It had been just another passing signpost in the Bath family's vagabond existence. But for Russell Rufus Bath, Murtho maintained importance as his birthplace. Throughout his teenage years, he often returned to sift through the ruins of its derelict houses and explore its cliffs, which were pockmarked with scores of caves - limestone caves.

12

MANIA

Since ancient times, tales of human petrification have inspired folklore, literature and poetry. Unsurprisingly when actual cases have come to light, they have generated extraordinary public interest.

The 17th-century story of a petrified miner called 'Fet-Matts' was a case in point. In 1677, Israelsson Matts from Falun in the Swedish province of Dalecarlia descended a deep shaft in the Falun copper mine to set blasting charges. He never returned. A massive blast killed nineteen miners and injured another dozen that day. Forty-seven years later, miners broke through a wall to find a dead man in old-fashioned clothes lying in 'vitriolic water'. The body appeared eerily fresh. When it was brought to the surface, an old woman, Margareta Olsdotter, came to the mine and recognised at once the body of Israelsson Matts, her former fiancé. Fet-Matts' petrified body was placed in a glass case in

Falun's Great Copper Mountain Mining Company Museum and left on display for tourists to view for the next thirty years. The body was then buried beneath the floor of the local church. When the floor was being repaired in 1860, Fet-Matts' remains were placed in a glass-covered coffin in the church gallery. In 1931, two hundred and fifty-four years after his death, Israelsson Matts finally received a proper churchyard burial.[13]

In the 19th century, petrified mania swept the world. Discoveries in the United States, Europe and Australia sparked scientific debate, sold newspapers and were often exploited for profit. And often, they told stories of a violent world where civilisations collided.

In 1892, the *Philadelphia Times* reported that labourers who were breaking new ground for a farm near Booneville, Colorado, had discovered the petrified body of a young, refined-looking Catholic priest clasping an ivory crucifix. The head of an arrow protruding from his chest told how he had met his death. His shoes were of a fashion worn in the latter part of the 17th century, at which time devoted Spanish missionaries were known to have visited the country to convert Indigenous populations to Catholicism.

---

[13] The case of the petrified Swedish miner inspired writers, poets and composers. The German romanticists, Ruckert and Hoffmann and the poet Archim von Arnim adapted his story. Composer, Richard Wagner drew up a preliminary plan for an opera in three acts.

The 19th-century discovery in South Australia of the petrified body of an Aboriginal man was a tale not only of a clash of civilisations but also of exploitation and greed.

In 1845 European settlers stumbled upon a series of limestone caves in South Australia that became known as the Naracoorte Caves. Soon after the discovery, news broke that explorers had found the body of an Indigenous man deep within one of the caves. It was thought that the man had entered the cave after becoming injured, then rested on a rock ledge, where he later died in a sleeping position. Newspapers suggested that he was the last of a party of Aboriginal people hunted down and shot by settlers in retaliation for killing one of their men and a sheep.

Seventeen years later, an Australian newspaper reported that the body of this petrified Aboriginal man had been sold at auction in London.

> On Tuesday, Mr J. C. Stevens, of King Street, Covent Garden, London, sold at auction a mummy or petrified Aboriginal of Australia found in a limestone cave at Mosquito Plains, South Australia.[14] It is the only specimen of its kind known to the scientific world. It is almost perfect in every detail and is believed to be of great antiquity. The bids began at £10/10/, and it was sold for £18/18/.[15]

---

[14] Naracoorte Caves and Mosquito Plains Caves are the same place.
[15] Adelaide *Register* May 14, 1866

The seller was an Adelaide showman by the name of Thomas Craig, who had stolen the petrified man, not once but twice.

On the first occasion, Craig had walked seventy miles from Mt Gambier to the Mosquito Plains, where he found the mouth of a limestone cave.

> Nervously he entered. Eureka! There lay the stone aboriginal in a posture of pain. The skin was a milky white. There had been no wasting in the figure, which was hard to the touch. Mr Craig wrapped a blanket around the exhibit, hoisted it onto his shoulder, and began the long, weary plod back to Mount Gambier.[16]

[16] Adelaide's *Mail* of December 5, 1953

On arrival at his hotel room, Craig stored the body under the bed. His aim was to exhibit it at carnivals. But following a tip-off, police alerted the Crown Lands Ranger, who confiscated the body and arranged for its repatriation to the cave, where it was placed behind specially installed bars as an exhibit for visitors. How such exploitation differed from the showman's odious aim was seemingly never contemplated.

But Mr Craig was not a man to be deterred. He later returned to the cave, where he breached the bars and absconded with the petrified man a second time.

This time, he fled to Sydney, where he put it on show. In their wisdom, the citizens of Sydney generally boycotted the exhibition.

Desperate for a return for his efforts, Craig secreted the body aboard a ship from Sydney to London, where it was sold at auction and subsequently exhibited at various locations around the city.

Throughout the 19th century, museums, carnival operators and wealthy individuals around the world offered large sums for petrified bodies, especially if a story and a name were attached to the body. Such was the demand that a unique black market evolved, serving buyers, sellers, grave robbers and fraudsters.

In the late 1880s, the petrified body of a one-eyed man was discovered in a limestone quarry in the Orange district of New South Wales. *'The Petrified Man of Cow Flat'* became an instant sensation. Shortly after the discovery, Mr W. Buchanan of Killarney Station, NSW, was said to have paid £1,000, an extraordinary sum for the time, to acquire it. But while in his possession, it was allegedly stolen and exhibited in Sydney.

Fierce controversy raged for months about how the petrification had taken place and whether or not *The Petrified Man of Cow Flat* was a hoax.

Dr W. H. McCarthy, a leading medical practitioner of the day, analysed portions of the arm and trunk and decided that petrification had occurred in a cave due to immersion in water heavily impregnated with lime. Analysis showed that phosphorous and other physiological elements were in precisely the same proportion as in the human body. The fact that the right leg was worn and withered in a manner which suggested that leg irons had once been attached to it, supported the theory that the body was originally that of a runaway convict who had escaped from a penal station in Sydney. It was thought that he had taken to the bush, where he lived with Aboriginals. While sheltering from a storm in the cave where his body was later found, he had likely become trapped by an earth fall. By the time his body was discovered, the petrification process was complete.

The story climaxed in the New South Wales Legislative Assembly when the Minister for Mines announced the result of a police investigation:

> Sub-inspector Ford of the Orange police reports: I have the honour to inform you that I have made very

careful inquiries about the so-called petrified man, said to have been found by G. F. Sala and son at the marble quarry at Caleula, about 15 miles from Orange. I am thoroughly convinced that the marble figure was made at Croaker's old public house at Cow Flat by G. F. Sala and that the marble was obtained from Bell's quarry, about two miles from Cow Flat.

I have obtained the following information - that Joseph Bell conveyed from his marble quarry, about five months since, a large piece of marble, about one-ton weight, to G. F. Sala's residence (Croaker's old public house), at Cow Flat and put it in out of the dray, halfway into the back kitchen, through the door; and Bell states that some 10 or 12 weeks afterwards he saw that a man had been modelled out of it by Sala and that he used acids; and whilst Sala was making the figure, his son Fred was always on the watch, and would at once whistle if any person came in sight, and that Sala would then come out of the kitchen, and shut the door.

The Petrified Man of Cow Flat was deemed a fraud, and the one-eyed figure's only value was as a curious sculpture.[17]

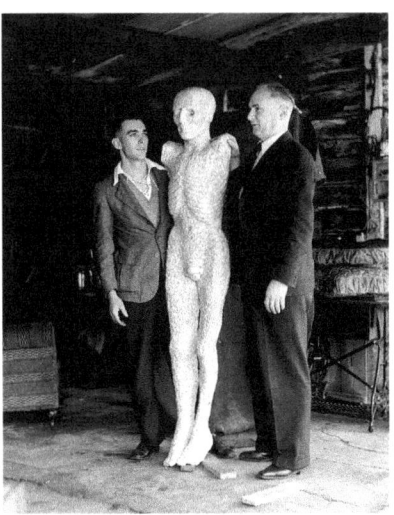

---

[17] In the 1930s, *The Petrified Man of Cow Flat* was exhibited at Bondi, New South Wales.

The editor of *The Echo* suggested the entire affair was 'illustrative of the inborn tendency of man to deceive and willingness of the world to be deceived.'

In the 19th century, newspapers both propagated and profited from the petrified mania that swept the world. In the United States, reportage of discoveries of petrified humans became so sensationalistic that newspaper editor Mark Twain satirised his journalistic colleagues' obsession with the phenomena.

> In the fall of 1862, in Nevada and California, the people got to running wild about extraordinary petrifactions and other natural marvels. One could scarcely pick up a paper without finding in it one or two glorified discoveries of this kind. I chose to kill the petrifaction mania with a very delicate satire. But maybe it was altogether too delicate, for nobody ever perceived the satire part of it at all.

By the mid-20th century, Australia's own petrified mania had subsided. The dreadful human carnage of two world wars explicitly delivered daily via newsreel screens had dampened the public's fascination with corpses.

And so it was that in 1951 when the case of the River Murray petrified body broke, local and interstate newspapers reports were invariably accurate and respectful. After all, this was a murder victim, and her killer needed to be brought to justice.

13

SNOOK

Detective David Flint had been chasing crooks and investigating crimes for two decades. His career began in Adelaide, but in the early 1940s, he was transferred to Renmark. Since then, he'd seen it all, from shop breaking and larceny to having to smash an opium den. In March 1950, a year before the mysterious body was found in the River Murray, Flint was appointed temporary officer in charge of Renmark Police Station following the sudden death of Sergeant T. Fitzgerald. But Flint's health was also deteriorating, and he collapsed at the Station a week later. He subsequently underwent surgery in Adelaide and took nine weeks off work to recover. Flint turned his thoughts to retirement, or at least a new phase in his life, as he liked to call it, as an orchardist and vegetable grower. Over the previous four years, Flint had been preparing a 38-acre block of land across the river from Renmark at Paringa. He spent his days off installing spray irrigation and transforming near-worthless land into productive acreage. But with still much to learn, he would often call on his neighbours and seek their advice on methods to improve his yield or field off pests.

On such a visit to a neighbour's property during The Petrified Woman investigation, he was approached by itinerant labourer Andy Peterson. Flint recognised him immediately. Four years back, Peterson and his friend, Roy Ray, had been on a rabbiting expedition in the back-country out from Renmark when their truck became bogged during a heavy thunderstorm. Peterson left Ray with the vehicle and set out to seek assistance. Somewhere along the way, Peterson took a wrong turn. When he failed to return, Ray walked to Renmark and reported Peterson's disappearance to the police. Detective Flint and a mounted constable immediately set off and searched a vast area. They were about to return to Renmark at nightfall when they found Peterson sheltering in a hut on Calperum Station, about 15 miles from Renmark. Peterson was grateful for the efforts of the police that day.

Peterson wiped soil from his hands, gave Flint a hearty handshake and said he remained in his debt. Flint smiled and said it was simply part of the job. He then joined the property owner for an inspection of his estate.

When Flint returned to his car an hour later, he found Andy Peterson crouched by the driver's door, rolling a cigarette. Peterson stood and said that he had some information possibly relevant to the missing woman case - information so prickly that he didn't want to go on record.

Flint was curious, "And what information would that be?"

Peterson looked a little sheepish as he mentioned a name, "Snook."

Snook was a well-known surname in Renmark's agricultural community. Flint had attended open days at James Snook's property on Seventh Street. He also knew his son, Eric - a bright kid who'd been wounded in New Guinea during the War.

"Which Snook? Jim or Eric?"

Peterson shook his head, "Neither. You want to talk to Jim's wife - or ex-wife, I should say - Lucy. She has information that might be helpful in the Bath case."

Peterson gave Flint an address and asked that his name not be mentioned.

The following morning, Flint pulled up at a timber-clad house on Renmark's Sixteenth Street, a few hundred yards from the home of Russell Bath's mother.

A slim woman in her early fifties came to the door. Her dark hair was freshly permed, and her lipstick a ruby red.

"Lucy Snook? I'm Detective Flint."

"And what am I supposed to have done now?" she barked.

"I understand you know a fellow named Russell Bath."

"Who's been gabbing about me?"

Flint took off his hat, wiped his shoes on the doormat and invited himself into her home.

Lucy Snook was born Lucy Jessie Hunt in South Australia on April 29, 1899. In her late teens, she'd had a series of run-ins with men, the first of which landed her in Court for using obscene language in a public place. The second incident involved a violent petty criminal with whom she'd cohabited, who landed her in Adelaide Hospital with severe injuries.

In 1921, she married James 'Jim' Henry Snook. The couple settled in Eighth Street, Renmark and had three children. But in June 1949, Jim suspected that Lucy was having an affair and employed the services of a private detective experienced in matrimonial investigations to track her movements. The private detective discovered that Mrs Snook was involved with not one but two local men - Ken Saunders and Atric Potter.

Lucy Snook

Jim Snook immediately filed for divorce. His solicitor publicised the circumstances in the city newspapers, naming Ken Saunders as the co-respondent. Lucy Snook didn't contest her husband's claim of infidelity, and a divorce was granted.

Saunders' wife also filed for divorce, naming Lucy Snook as the co-respondent. This was decades before 'no-fault' divorce was brought in Australia, and significant humiliation was guaranteed for any co-respondent in a divorce case.

Flint removed his hat and asked Lucy, "I understand that you have information that could assist our investigation into the disappearance of Margaret Salter, or Mrs Bath as she was known in Renmark."

"Is that right? Who told you this? Bloody Andy Peterson?"

Flint asked her to calm down, take a seat and tell him what she knew.

Renmark was a small town, she said, and she'd found herself in the company of Bath and Marg at the Renmark Hotel on occasion.

Then, in July 1950, barely three months after Margaret's disappearance, Russell Bath had sidled up to her at the Hotel.

"Russell told me Marg had left him, and he said she was fed up with being out-back. He told me how he drove her to Renmark, and how she suddenly got out there. He said she's been seen in Melbourne and also in Mildura."

Snook's testimony fitted Bath's version of events, minus the black Chevrolet.

"Anything else you want to add?"

"Not really." She said sheepishly.

"If you'd like to get something off your chest, I'd suggest you do it now or accompany me down to the Station."

She got up and walked to a sideboard, where she took a cigarette and lit it.

"Russell said he had a car and offered to take two girlfriends and me dancing and drinking."

She said they took advantage of the offer.

"He started to drive me down to my daughter's place at Loxton, too."

Snook said that he then took her to his place at Lindsay Point. In fact, she went with him several times.

"One time, he used a boat moored near his back door on Lindsay Creek. He rowed me about six miles upriver to the Stewarts' place to visit them. And when we were alone in the dining room, he put it on me."

"By that, you mean?"

"We had sexual intercourse there, but I wasn't happy about it, really. That was October 1950. We were also intimate in the car on several occasions when he used to take me to Loxton to see my daughter."

Lucy Snook told Flint that around Christmas 1950, seven months after Marg allegedly left him, Bath asked her to become his housekeeper at Lindsay Point. He said that if it worked out, he would marry her. Unknown to Snook, this was precisely the modus operandi he'd used to woo Margaret Salter. And there were other similarities - Lucy was also a divorcee and much older than Bath.

"I didn't like him that much, and from the outset, I said 'no' to becoming his housekeeper. Then, one day at the Hotel, he suggested we get engaged! He showed me an engagement ring and said, 'Marg gave me back the ring.' And I said, 'It'll have to be a new ring,' and he said, 'I'll take you to a shop.' I hardly knew him!"

Snook admitted using Bath to her advantage but with increasing unease.

"One time recently, when coming back from Loxton, he said, 'What is it about me that you don't like?' I said, 'I can't fathom you out.' He said, 'Go on.' And I said, 'You are unobliging, selfish, and there is something evil about you.'"

Snook said that she eased herself out of the relationship by saying that she was seeing another Renmark man, Andy Peterson. A few months later, Snook's name was again in the newspapers - this time as the co-respondent in Peterson's divorce.

Flint told her that she would likely be required to appear at a Coronial Inquest. That was all she needed - more publicity about her twisted love life - and now her involvement with an alleged murderer! It was more than her battered reputation could take.

14

BROTHER

According to old timers, the Bath clan had had a chequered relationship with the law. Detective Flint did some digging around town and reviewed Police and Court records, desperately searching for any information that might assist the Adelaide detectives running the case.

He discovered that Russell Bath was one of nine siblings, and that the first seven children, including Russell, had been born in humpies and tents on different properties in different districts. Just before the outbreak of the First World War, the Bath family finally settled in Renmark, then a town of eight hundred residents, where Russell Bath Snr found steady work on the River Murray's man-made locks.

In November 1923, the two eldest Bath sons, William and Vivian, and another youth were arrested for breaking into a shop at Millicent and stealing goods valued at £30, which they had put in a boat and rowed down the River Murray.

Appearing in the Supreme Court, the judge stated that there was a previous conviction against Vivian Bath for stealing goods from a river steamer. The judge sentenced all three men to prison for fifteen months with hard labour.

In 1933, the youngest Bath son, Henry, was prosecuted for hunting at Woolenook Bend with an unlicensed gun.

During the Second World War, the wider Bath family was spread across South Australia, western Victoria and New South Wales, and boasted sixty men serving in the fighting forces. Three of Russell's brothers, Harry, Vivian and Charlie, had volunteered. Russell had also volunteered but he failed his literacy and aptitude tests. He was the only one of the four brothers the military rejected.

Harry, Vivian and Charlie Bath served overseas in the Australian Infantry Forces. Harry and Charlie were wounded in action, and Vivian was posted as missing in Malaya. At the War's end, Russell Bath's three brothers returned home and soon found employment on pastoral properties along the River Murray.

Flint decided to follow up on Humphrey Kempe's suggestion that he speak with Charlie Bath, Russell's closest brother. Charlie was a bachelor who lived and worked at Millewa, the neighbouring sheep and cattle property east of Lindsay Point, which Humphrey Kempe had previously owned.

Two years back, Charlie had been charged with public drunkenness. But compared with his brothers, he was a clean skin. Charlie's only other known contact with the police had been in 1946 following his discovery of the body of fifty-two-year-old Victor Tillett in swampy bushland beside the River Murray.

Tillett, the Secretary of the Renmark Irrigation Trust, had been missing for two days when Charlie Bath found him, a revolver in his hand and a bullet through his forehead. Allegedly, Tillett had been suffering from depression before his disappearance.

Victor Tillett lived only a hundred yards from where Charlie was then residing with his parents in Renmark. Indeed, the Bath and Tillet homes backed onto the same laneway. It was strangely coincidental that Charlie should have discovered his neighbour's body under a bush in swampy land a mile and a half from their homes.

Detective David Flint had investigated the incident and found no evidence that any other person was implicated in Tillett's death.

———

Flint contacted the Victorian Police, who despatched First Constable Weston to the Millewa property to interview Charlie Bath. Millewa's owner advised Weston that the flood had left Charlie's hut knee-high in water and mud, so he was now staying at fisherman Dan O'Connell's shack on higher ground.

Constable Weston arrived at O'Connell's hut to find Charlie blind drunk. According to O'Connell, Charlie had been drinking since before breakfast.

What Charlie told the Constable was astonishing. He said that his brother Russell had told him about Marg's disappearance, and had insinuated that she was dead and that the body found in the river was hers. Charlie said he'd advised Russell not to admit to what he had done, even if they threw tables and chairs at him.

Charlie's testimony left little doubt in Constable Watson's mind that the body of the petrified woman was that of Margaret Salter.

———

On December 4, 1951, nine weeks into the investigation, Detective Flint and Detective Inspector Gully from Adelaide and Detective Harper from Melbourne initiated a coordinated attempt to force Russell Bath to confess to the murder of Margaret Salter.

Together, they travelled to the Lindsay Point property, bundled Russell Bath into their vehicle and drove to the gate leading to neighbouring Millewa Station.

> With Russell Bath, we returned to the Road Junction into Millewa Station, where we interviewed Russell Bath, who is an uneducated, cunning individual of low intelligence. Practically everything of importance concerning the disappearance of Mrs Salter and the finding of the body was put to him. But his low animal cunning made it most difficult to converse with him. When we came to a point where he was in difficulties,

he would either not answer or say, "I have nothing further to say."

Simultaneously, Victorian detectives had swooped on Millewa Station and collected Russell's brother Charlie from Dan O'Connell's hut and driven him to the Road Junction. Their aim was to interview the brothers together and have Charlie repeat what Russell had told him. But Charlie was again in 'a drunken condition, having consumed a quantity of wine.' When the detectives couldn't get any sense out of him, they had no choice but to return him to Millewa.

The detectives then drove Russell Bath to Werrimull Police Station, where he was interrogated again in the presence of Detective Inspector Gully and Detectives Harper and Flint and Detective Inspector Donnelly, Victoria's Chief of the Homicide Squad.

"A number of things you told Gully and Mr Harper have been checked, and it appears that you did not tell the truth."

"I am not going to say anything more about that."

"We have every reason to believe that the body found in the Murray River in September this year is that of Mrs Salter."

"I don't want to say anything about that."

"You told the detectives that a number of people had seen Mrs Salter since she disappeared. Can you give us any definite information about any person who saw her alive after she left Lindsay Point station where you were living?"

"No, only what I have heard."

"We heard that there is an unsigned letter that you say you got from West Australia."

"I lost it. I don't know where it is now."

"What was in the letter?"

"Only that she was seen in West Australia."

"I understood from you that you told the detectives that the letter was from Mrs Salter."

"It could have been."

"Well, was it her handwriting? You would know her writing."

"It could have been. I haven't had much education."

"You would know whether it was from her or not?"

"I thought it was from her."

"What was in the letter?"

"Only that she was supposed to be seen in West Australia."

"She would not be writing saying that she was seen in West Australia, would she?"

"I forget what was in the letter."

"How long after her disappearance did you see the letter?"

"A good long time, months, I suppose."

"Where was the letter delivered?"

"Lindsay Point Station."

"Did you tell Mr Kempe or any other person on the Lindsay Point Station about it?"

"No."

"Why not?"

"I didn't bother."

"According to you, Mrs Price of Mildura saw Mrs Salter after her disappearance."

"Yes, I hear she saw her."

"Is that the Mrs Price whose husband is a friend of your brother Charlie and Harry?"

"Yes, he is a relative of ours."

"Is he the man who brings the wine up to your brother?"

"He brings a drop up to the brothers."

"According to your brother Charlie, he brought up the wine that he got drunk on this morning."

"Yes, they get stuck into it as soon as he brings it up."

"Did you try to trace Mrs Salter where you believe you heard she might be?"

"No, why should I?"

"You know what the people in the district are saying about you?"

"Yes, they all reckon I killed her."

"Why didn't you try to find her if you heard of her in so many places."

"I don't want to say any more about that."

"Detective Inspector Gully and Sergeant Harper of Adelaide have interviewed a lot of people since the disappearance of Mrs Salter, and a lot of stories you have told do not appear to be the truth. Can you give any definite information about her?"

"This has worried me ever since. I know what people are saying, and I would like to have it cleared up, and I would like to see a lawyer."

"Why do you want to see a solicitor?"

"What I have told you and the men from Adelaide is not true, and if I see a lawyer and he tells me to tell the truth, I will do it, and I think it will not be so bad as people say, and it will be better for me."

"Well, why not tell us the truth now?"

"No, take me to a lawyer, and if he says for me to tell the truth, I will."

"Who would you like to see?"

"Mr Favalora in Mildura."

Around 9 pm, the detectives met Mr Favalora at his Mildura office. Fifteen minutes later, Russell Bath arrived and held a private interview with Mr Favalora.

Mr Favalora then called the detectives back into his office.

"He will make a statement on the lines which he told the Police that she left him in Renmark."

Detective Inspector Donnelly said, "He has already told the Police that story, and he told us today that story was not true and that he wanted to consult you as to telling a true story."

Sitting with his head down, Bath didn't respond.

Inspector Donnelly said to Bath, "You have got us here under false pretences. I am satisfied that Mr Favalora would not advise you to tell untruths, and it would appear that you do not trust him."

Mr Favalora asked the detectives to leave the room again to allow him to speak with his client.

Afterwards, Mr Favalora told the police, "Mr Bath tells me that he's not going to give you anything different."

The detectives returned Bath to the Mildura Police Station and asked if he had any complaints to make about his treatment. Bath said, "No."

The police record of the meeting suggests that Bath's solicitor had attempted to convince him to admit to killing Margaret, but in doing so, had undermined any chance of a confession.

> He was taken to Mr Favalora's office in Mildura, where he no doubt became suspicious of Mr Favalora, who was ready and willing to advise him to tell the whole truth or nothing at all. Bath then resorted to his former story about her leaving him on April 14, 1950, at Renmark Railway Station. He was advised again by Mr Favalora, who co-operated with us in an endeavour to obtain the true facts, but Bath attempted to adhere to his former story.

Bath was released and departed the police station with his sister's husband.

The investigation had stalled. The detectives felt they'd been close to cracking the case, but Bath had simply played them. Their counter move was to delay the Coronial Inquest as long as possible, to let Bath stew and possibly crack.

Adelaide detectives met with Harry Salter to advise him that he would be called as a witness at the Inquest, which would likely not take place for another six months. The delay prompted doubts in his mind that his mother's fate would ever be established and her killer brought to justice.

According to his daughter, Margaret Ellis, uncertainty gave way to fear one evening in early 1952.

> We had been to my other grandmother's place that night. It was only mum, my sister and myself. It was dark, and we were coming home, and somebody was following us down the street. We had low gates, and my mother jumped over the gate, and by the time we got to the front door, he was standing out the front of our house. We thought it could have been Russell. Not having a phone, we couldn't ring the police. When Dad got home, mum told him. He turned around, went to the police and told them that somebody had been standing out the front of our house and giving us a bit of a scare.

15

UNKNOWN-UNKNOWN

On November 5, 1951, after six weeks stored at the Adelaide City Morgue, the body of the petrified woman was laid to rest in a pauper's grave at Adelaide's West Terrace Cemetery, under warrant from the Renmark Coroner. No mourners were present to witness the interment, and there was no priest to bless her on her journey into the afterworld.

She shared the grave with a 66-year-old Swedish-born itinerant worker, who had been buried seventeen days earlier, and with two unnamed infants who had been interred back in the mid-1880s. A month after her burial, the body of a 79-year-old man, who'd spent more than half a century in an Adelaide asylum, was interred in the same grave.

No gravestone or plaque named the occupants. In the mortuary records, the petrified woman was registered simply as 'Unknown-Unknown'.

As fate would have it, gravediggers elsewhere would soon be preparing a plot for the burial of a vital witness in the petrified woman case.

16

I'LL SHOOT MYSELF

By April 1952, the River Murray floodwaters had subsided, but Charlie Bath was still bunking down with fisherman Daniel O'Connell on higher ground at Millewa Station. Dan and Charlie had known each other since childhood and shared a love of hunting and alcohol.

On Saturday, the 26th of April, they drove together to Renmark to buy supplies of wine and beer. Charlie also picked up a copy of the Murray Pioneer newspaper. On their return to Millewa Station late that afternoon, they began a heavy drinking session with Charlie's nephew, Ted Casey, who also lived nearby on the Millewa property.

In the early evening, Dan O'Connell browsed the newspaper and noticed the front page story about the upcoming Inquest into the death of the unknown woman found floating in the river. After reading it, he handed it to Charlie, who browsed it and exclaimed, "If they hang him, they'll hang me!"

According to Dan, "Charlie was very excited and started to cry."

The following Friday evening, Charlie had another heavy drinking session with Dan, his nephew Ted, and Reg Anspach, also a labourer at Millewa Station. Dan woke at 5 am on Saturday to find Charlie still up, talking with his nephew Ted in the kitchen.

Later that morning, after Ted departed, Dan went out to check his rabbit traps. On his return, Charlie asked him to lend him his rifle.

Dan asked, "What do you want it for?"

Charlie replied, "I want to blow my brains out."

Dan said, "Get out, don't be silly, I'll throw it into the creek - you don't mean that."

Charlie dared Dan to do just that. Realising that Charlie was possibly serious about killing himself, Dan retrieved the rifle from his bedroom, went outside and threw it in the creek. On his return to the hut, he sat down and rolled himself a cigarette. He noticed Charlie finish his glass of wine and stand up, but didn't see where he went.

Dan's next recollection was the sound of a shotgun blast from just outside the hut. He went outside and found Charlie lying near a tree, his body quivering. He was fully dressed, but his right foot was bare. A boot and a sock were laying nearby. He had a hole in the right side of his head and neck. A large pool of blood flowed toward the creek. The shotgun barrel was smeared with blood and pointed towards his head.

Dan O'Connell drove to the Millewa homestead to raise the alarm. At 8.30 that evening, Police Constable John Killeen from Mildura arrived, examined Charlie and confirmed that 'life was extinct'.

In his witness deposition, Dan O'Connell stated that there had been no one else in the vicinity besides himself when the deadly shot was fired. He said that Charlie had become upset after reading about the upcoming Inquest and cried. O'Connell stated that he'd never seen Charlie cry before.

"He said, 'Everything was over.'"

After speaking with Daniel O'Connell, Constable Killeen believed that there were no suspicious circumstances surrounding the death of Charles Bath.

Constable Killeen also interviewed Millewa Station labourer Reg Anspach, who said that the day before Charlie Bath's death, they'd travelled together to Renmark to buy drinks. He said that Charlie also purchased a bandage for troublesome ulcers on his leg that had plagued him since the War.

"I advised him to go see a doctor about his leg. He replied, 'It will be straight into an ambulance and Dawes Road Hospital.' By that, he meant the Military Hospital. He then said, 'I'll cure it myself - I'll shoot myself.' I said, 'Don't be silly.' He then laughed."

Ted Casey testified that he noticed his Uncle Charlie was upset by the article in the *Murray Pioneer*. Ted explained that he had spent the evening drinking and talking with the deceased. But Ted chose not to divulge what they had discussed.

Charlie Bath's suicide two days before the Inquest was a stunning development. His statement, "If they hang him, they'll hang me," implied that Russell Bath was implicated in the death of Margaret and that Charlie was either directly involved in her death, had been a witness to her killing or had helped dispose of her body.

Intriguingly, Charlie Bath chose the identical method to take his own life as had the secretary of the Renmark

Irrigation Trust, Victor Tillet, whose body Charlie had found five years earlier.

As for Russell Bath's reaction to his brother's suicide? He simply disappeared.

Man found shot dead

RENMARK, Mon.: The body of Charles Bath, garden employe. of Millewa, was found during the week-end on property where he was employed.

He had been shot through the head. A 12-gauge gun was lying alongside the body.

Bath. who was a member of a well-known family in the Upper Murray districts, was a returned serviceman from World War II.

17

CIRCUS

On Monday, May 5, 1952, reporters, locals and nosey out-of-towners lined the street outside Renmark Courthouse, hoping to gaze on the procession of witnesses called to testify in a case that had garnered Australia-wide interest. Some locals applauded David Flint as he alighted from his car. Four months earlier, he'd retired after twenty-three years in the South Australia Police Force.

The Coroner, Mr Hurtle Horace Hobcroft, entered the Court to find two frazzled detectives conferring in whispered tones with the police representative at the Inquest, Sergeant Ward.

Ward stood, apologised to the Coroner and called for an adjournment of proceedings to enable police to locate a vital witness who had not appeared - Russell Rufus Bath. The crowded Court erupted, with the newspaper men from Adelaide and Melbourne the most vocal. With the chief

Renmark Court House

suspect in the case missing, the Coroner had no option but to grant an adjournment.

The following day, *The Chronicle* newspaper reported on the fiasco:

> Police are searching for Russell Rufus Bath, station hand, formerly of Lindsay Point station, who is wanted as a witness in an Inquest into the death of an unknown woman whose body was recovered from the River Murray at Renmark last October. The Inquest was set down for yesterday but was not opened by the Renmark Coroner (Mr H. H. Hobcroft) because police had been unable to locate Bath. Bath's brother, Charles Bath, station hand of Millewa Station, was found on Saturday shot dead in a hut on the station, situated on Lindsay Creek, about 13 miles from Lindsay Point station.

Detectives and police officers, some of whom had travelled hundreds of miles from Adelaide and Melbourne to appear at the Inquest, were furious. David Flint, too, was aghast - this was one of the most high-profile cases during his time in Renmark. Where was the police oversight? It was, without doubt, a Victorian Police matter to ensure Russell Bath appeared at the Inquest, but Flint was convinced this debacle wouldn't have happened had he delayed his own retirement.

Two days later, Russell Bath presented himself to Mildura Police, claiming that he hadn't been informed about the date of the Inquest.

Three weeks later, the Inquest resumed at the Renmark Courthouse. To avoid the press, Bath's lawyer Mr Pickering ushered him in via a rear door and to a front row seat to the right of the dock. Wearing a brown suit with an open neck white shirt, he gave a momentary glance around the room. There were faces he knew, people he considered friends. Were they there to support him or rat on him?

Once seated, Bath felt the eyes of all present burning the back of his neck. He knew he was centerstage - suspected of murder. But he was sharing the spotlight with another - the mysterious petrified woman - a murder victim, whom the police were certain was his de facto wife, Margaret Salter.

Coroner Mr Hobcroft entered the Court, took his seat and began proceedings.

Irrigation worker Charlie Wilson was the first witness called. He gave a detailed account of his discovery of the body floating in the River Murray. He was followed by Detective David Flint, who told of retrieving the body.

Adelaide Detective Harper then provided a detailed précis of the police investigation and post-mortem results. Harper stated that he was present on September 29, 1951, when police pathologist, Dr J. M. Dwyer, carried out a post-mortem examination on the body. Dwyer had found a fracture on the left side of the skull, which he concluded had occurred before death. In the Doctor's opinion, death had occurred twelve to eighteen months before the body was found. The body, he said, was in a state of fatty-calcification.

Harper explained that Dwyer's description of the body, regarding her age, height and general build, fitted that of Margaret Salter.

Harper then read the transcript of the initial interview with Russell Bath at Lindsay Point Station. Harper said that while the interview was in progress, former detective David Flint carried out a search of Russell Bath's home and found blood on linoleum, which Bath claimed had seeped from an old refrigerator. The stains on the linoleum, Harper said, were subsequently examined by clinical pathologist Dr J. A. Bonnin at the Institute of Medical and Veterinary Science, and determined to be human blood.

Harper then revealed that two women related to Bath had alleged sightings of Margaret Salter in the months following her disappearance, but that neither woman could confirm that the person they saw had been Margaret Salter.

Harper said that despite descriptions of Margaret Salter being widely publicised in newspapers throughout the Commonwealth no one else had come forward with information regarding her whereabouts. However, under cross-examination by Bath's legal representative, Mr Pickering, Detective Harper conceded that it had not been possible to identify the body as that of Margaret Salter.

The Inquest then heard from fruit grower Donald Bruce, a resident of Renmark who had visited the Baths at Lindsay Point. Bruce revealed that Bath had said, "Marg was going through the 'change of life'; she was very nervous and upset and would wake up through the night…."

Bruce recalled Bath telling him that she wanted to go on a holiday, and "in the morning, he ran her down to Renmark, and there was a big black sedan car there. And she went away in this car. Just before she went, she said, 'This is where we part.' And he gave her half his money - £140 - to help her along."

Bruce confirmed that he had asked Mr Bath if they had had an argument.

"He said there was an argument over relations.[18] He said he thought it could come right. There was no mention of anyone hitting anyone, and there is nothing I can add regarding the argument over relations."

Half a dozen other witnesses were called at the Inquest, including Lucy Snook.

She testified: "About four to five months after she had dis-appeared, it was suggested to me (by Russell Bath) that I keep house. He asked me to keep house for him at Lindsay Point. I could go up for 3 to 6 months and see how I liked it. He suggested that we become engaged. He showed me rings, and they were Margaret's. He did not offer me a ring for an engagement ring. I said I would not be engaged to him. In April 1951, Mr Bath gave me a brooch. He said he bought it in Adelaide. I was rather dubious about whether it was new or not...."

Lucy Snook also testified that Bath told her Marg was in the Victorian town of Stawell, working in a business. She also recalled him telling her that he'd received a letter from

---

[18] Relatives of Russell Bath.

Marg from Western Australia, in which she said she would never come back.

Kenneth Thomas 'Bill' Phillips, the manager of Tareena station, recalled Russell Bath arriving at his home the day Margaret disappeared.

"He was not quite himself. He was a little morose. He said that Marg had had a nervous breakdown and she had gone away for a spell."

Questioned about the presence of limestone in the district, Phillips said he didn't know of any limestone at Lindsay Point, but recalled telling detectives about the location of limestone caves at Wilkinsons Cliffs at Murtho in South Australia.

All eyes were on the final witness Russell Bath as he entered the witness box. He gave his current address as Sixteenth Street, Renmark.

Inspector Bonython, who represented South Australia's Police Commissioner, asked Bath whether he had lived with a woman known as Margaret Salter.

Bath looked to the Coroner and replied, "I decline to answer any questions on the advice of my solicitor."

In his final summation, the Coroner found that the River Murray victim's body was that of a woman, probably over forty-five, whose identity had not been disclosed by the evidence. In his opinion, death was likely caused by a fractured skull. He said that he would forward the depositions to the Crown Solicitor in Adelaide for consideration.

There is no record of the Crown Solicitor's opinion on the case, but we know that no further investigation was pursued.

Crown Solicitor To Study Testimony

Verdict At Inquest Fails To Identify Body In Limestone

ADELAIDE, Sat.—An inquest at Renmark this week did not establish the identity of a woman whose body, encased by a freak of nature in a limestone shell, was found in River Murray mudflats near the Victorian border in September.

The Melbourne *Herald* encapsulated the inconclusive outcome with the headline:

STONE WOMAN REMAINS A MYSTERY.

By the end of the summer of 1953, wild grass had grown knee-high over the burial site of the petrified woman. Bereft of a gravestone, a passerby would have been forgiven for trampling on her final resting place.

Officialdom had decided that she and the other souls with whom she shared the pauper's grave were best forgotten.

The Petrified Woman

18

FEUD

In 2017, I was commissioned by a local production company to research and write scripts for a true crime animation series, *Twist*.[19] While researching historical cases for the series, I found a newspaper article about the petrified woman case. The story didn't fit the series brief, but I decided to dig deeper into this intriguing unsolved case.

I accessed Coronial records, which included the Police Department's brief on the case and witness statements. I then began looking for people mentioned in the reports and in newspapers. The events took place more than six decades ago, and everyone I researched - the detectives, witnesses and family members - were either untraceable or had long since died.

But by a circuitous route using a genealogy website, electoral records and the telephone directory, I tracked

---

[19] Produced for Broken Yellow Production and the Australian Broadcasting Corporation.

down a woman by the name of Patricia Margaret Ellis who went by the name of Margaret. Now in her late 70s, she was Harry Salter's daughter and Margaret Salter's closest living relative. She was surprised and delighted to hear of my interest in the woman she called 'Grandma Bath'.

She told me that in 1950, when she was eight years old, she spent part of the Christmas school holidays with her grand-mother and Russell Bath. She said they had picked her up from the family home in Adelaide and driven her in Russell Bath's car up to Lindsay Point.

> I had a fabulous time. She was great, and we got on like a house on fire. She was always bubbly, and I always got hugs from her - a soft, gentle woman who never spoke harshly to anyone. And I always had a good time every time I was up there. Russell Bath was her only partner that I knew of. He was good to me and played games with me. He always treated my grandmother well, except when they had arguments, of course. They used to have their arguments, but they were never violent. Put it this way, he must have been on his best behaviour while I was there. When I was not there, you never know.

She told me that in 1951 when *The Petrified Woman* story broke, her father took her aside:

"He said he'd been to the police, and they wanted me to give a statement in case it ever went to Court. So he took me to the Police Station, and I told them what I knew."

For any child, the prospect of a police interview might be daunting. But she told them her recollections of her last holiday at Lindsay Point Station, four months before her grandmother's disappearance.

"I said they had an argument the last time I was there, and it was a strong argument. But I couldn't remember what it was about."

At my first face-to-face meeting with Margaret Ellis, she related on camera an extraordinary detail, which, had her father revealed it to the police at the time, might well have led to the ident-ification of the petrified woman.

> According to my father, the person who could have identified the body never did, and that was my Uncle Ted's wife, Jessamine Salter. She and Grandma were in a car accident together, and Grandma had a scar from this accident. But Jessamine didn't come forward to identify it.

As mentioned earlier, within days of the case becoming public, Mrs Eva Edge, a widow of Norwood in Adelaide, had contacted the police. She had told them that Margaret Salter was involved in a motor lorry accident in 1935 on Mount Barker Road, near Mount Hut, and that one of her legs was severely scarred by barbed wire. She had nursed Mrs Salter at her home and believed she could identify the scars the pathologist found on the right thigh of the corpse.

Mrs Edge even had photos of the injured leg. But the police weren't convinced that identification by this method alone would be enough to sway a Coroner, and so, remarkably, they turned down Mrs Edge's offer to view the body.[20]

Had Jessamine Salter gone to the police with an offer to identify the scarring, as had Mrs Eva Edge, the case may have been quickly resolved. But as Margaret Ellis explained, her aunt refused to go to the police because of a bitter family breakdown over religion.

"My father was a very strict Catholic, and his brother Ted married Jessamine in an Anglican Church - so my father refused to go to the wedding."

---

[20] The police believed the marks came about due to the body being placed on a wire bed, despite no evidence found to back that theory.

The feud had escalated three years later, in 1939, when Ted Salter died suddenly at the age of twenty-six, and Harry Salter refused to attend his funeral. From that day on, Ted's widow, Jessamine, wanted nothing to do with the Salter family. Indeed, Jessamine's son, Ted Jnr, whom I located during my research, knew nothing about his grandmother, let alone about her mysterious death.

And so it was that a bitter estrangement between the dead woman's sons over religion foiled an opportunity to identify the petrified woman as Margaret Salter, and her killer walked free.

19

BREAK POINT

Throughout my career as a documentary filmmaker, I have investigated numerous unsolved crime and espionage cases. And when searching for clues, I've learned to heed Sherlock Holme's advice: "Nothing is more deceptive than the obvious."

In *The Petrified Woman* case, the original investigators always believed that the victim was Margaret Salter. Indeed, there was no evidence to suggest that the victim was not Russell Bath's missing fifty-nine-year-old de facto wife. Unfortunately, the investigators couldn't determine why she was murdered, where she was killed, or the instrument used.

The police pathologist suggested that she had been struck with a blunt instrument. When a stain found on linoleum flooring at Russell Bath's home proved to be human blood, the investigators assumed she had been killed there and moved to a hide-out along the River Murray. But in time, the police began to have doubts about this scenario.

> The probabilities are that Bath killed her at the house, but on the other hand, when interrogating Bath, it was obvious he was exceptionally confident (that this wasn't the case), so much so that all members of the Force who spoke with him had the feeling that the killing may not have occurred in the house.

So where did he do it? And what was the motive?

I believe the witness statements reveal both the 'where' and the 'why'.

Margaret's son, Harry Salter, told detectives that the last time he saw her, she said to him, "I will go silly if I have to go up to the property further up the Murray as Russell has been asked to do. I don't want to go. I want him to come to Adelaide and get a job, but he won't."

During Detective Harper's first interview with Bath, he asked,

"Over what period was this talk of her leaving you?"

Bath replied, "It was about three months."

During the interview, Bath said that Margaret's relations, the Breens, were staying at Lindsay Point, and on the night of the 13th of April, he and Margaret had entertained them. The guests knew they were heading off on holiday the following day, the 14th of April.

Margaret's grandnephew John Breen confirmed to detectives that his family was indeed living at Lindsay Point at the time. He also confirmed that he knew of Russell and Margaret's holiday plans and told detectives that the couple would have left early in the morning of the 14th of April.

When the police questioned Russell Bath, he consistently swore that they departed Lindsay Point in his Packard car that morning at around 5 am. He said Margaret wore a linen house frock and a full rabbit skin coat. In mid-autumn and at the coldest hour of the morning, a thick coat would certainly have been required.

Each time Bath was questioned, Renmark Railway Station figured centrally in his version of events. He claimed that they arrived at the Station around 6 am - and that it was dark. Records confirm that sunrise was at 6.38 that morning, and the train to Adelaide was scheduled to depart Renmark Railway Station at 7.30 am.

Renmark Railway Station

When Bath claimed that Margaret got out of his Packard at the Railway Station and into a Chevrolet, his story clearly veered into the fictional. Indeed, while he told most people, including his friend Don Bruce, that the Chevrolet that mysteriously pulled up was black, he told Bruce's wife that the Chevrolet was cream.

But I believe that there was a reason for them to stop at Renmark Railways Station, and it was made clear in a number of witness statements.

In Don Bruce's interview with detectives, he recalled Bath saying to him that he and Margaret were arguing over her relatives and she had said, "You better drive me to Renmark."

In Lucy Snook's statement, she testified:

"He said to me that she had become fed up with being outback and that he had driven her to Renmark. From what I understood from him, they talked about it the night before, and she wanted to go, and he drove her into Renmark. He never told me about going to the Festival in the Barossa Valley. He never mentioned the black car to me. I thought she was going by train when he said, 'I brought her to the Station.'"

In his second Police interview, Bath essentially confirmed Snook's version of events when Detective Harper asked, "Did you resent her telling you that she was going to leave you?"

To which Bath replied, "I was very fond of her and did not want her to go."

"Was there any argument before she left?"

"I am not going to tell you anything further."

Bath's responses imply both a determination on Margaret's part to leave him and a strong possibility that they had argued about it.

Bath also admitted that there had been previous discussions about her desire to leave him when Detective Harper pressed him a second time, "Over what period had you two been discussing breaking it up?"

Bath answered, "Over a few weeks, two or three weeks…. And she decided to take a break of three months for a start and then probably come back."

"What was finally decided upon between you?" asked Harper.

"At last, she said she would not come back."

Bath admitted that Margaret was ending their eleven-year relationship, thus negating his former claim that they were heading off on holidays together.

"When was it that you left Lindsay Point together?" probed Detective Gully.

"On the 14th of April, 1950 was the climax. She was nervous and wanted a break, and under the circumstances, I was prepared for her to go."

"Were you prepared for her to come back?"

"I wanted her to come back."

Did Bath agree to let her go, but on arrival at the Renmark Railway Station, change his mind and lash out at her?

20

THRUST

If we presume Bath killed Margaret at Renmark Railway Station, how did he do it? Bath may have assaulted Margaret outside the car, but the danger of being seen by a passerby makes this an unlikely scenario. It's far more likely that they argued inside the car. The pathologist's sketch reveals a fracture on the left side of the victim's head.

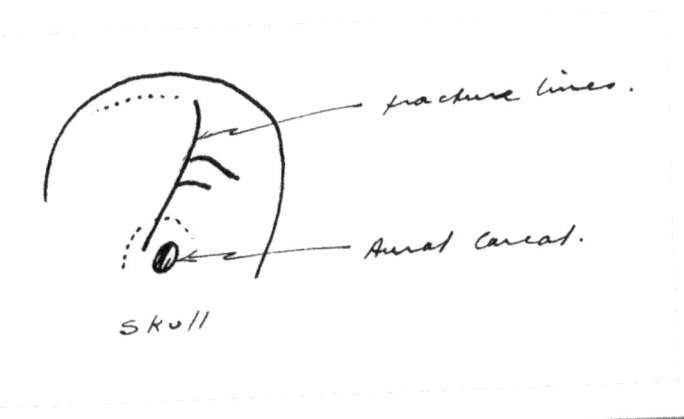

In Australian Packard sedans, the driver is seated on the right, and the passenger to the driver's left. Since Bath was seated on the right side of Margaret, the use of a blunt instrument to attack from inside the car can be ruled out. But if Bath thrust her head violently against the central doorframe or the quarter window - which was standard on most Packard models of the 1930s and 40s - the point of impact would match the fracture she suffered to the left side of her skull.

There is little doubt in my mind that Margaret Salter was dead before or around daybreak. But was it murder or manslaughter?

Bath may not have intended to kill Margaret. In fact, he implied as much late in his second police interview when he asked to see a solicitor.

Inspector Donnelly had asked, "Why do you want to see a solicitor?"

Bath replied, "What I have told you and the men from Adelaide is not true, and if I see a lawyer and he tells me to tell the truth, I will do it, and I think it will not be so bad as people say, and it will be better for me."

Indeed, if found guilty of the lesser charge of manslaughter, Bath would likely have faced a lengthy prison term rather than the hangman's noose.

21

CAVE

The Police Pathologist, Dr J.M. Dwyer, suggested that the calcified state of the body indicated burial in damp calcareous, i.e. limestone, rich soil. There is no known limestone-rich soil on or near Lindsay Point Station. But several people interviewed said the nearest area with limestone was the system of caves beneath cliffs on the River Murray at Murtho, over the border into South Australia.

Bill Phillips, the manager of Tareena Station, told detectives about the location of the caves:

"I know the country and the River around Woolenook Bend, and Russell Bath would also know the country. The only limestone country upriver from Woolenook Bend is around Wilkinson's Cliffs in S.A., and the Murtho Road runs close to these cliffs. There are caves in this area, and when the river is in flood, the water would reach these caves. All the cliffs are on the southern side of the river."

Unknown to the police at the time, their suspect, Russell Bath, had been born in Murtho and lived much of his adult life within twenty miles of the settlement. As Bath was unlikely to have left Lindsay Point with a shovel in his car to dig a grave, a cave would have offered an obvious solution for immediate disposal of a body.

Two weeks into the investigation, Detective Gully postulated the cave theory in his report:

> I believe that the body is that of Margaret Salter. She had been threatening to leave Bath for about three months prior to her disappearance, but he still wanted her with him. I suspect that Bath struck Salter over the head and killed her when the final break between them came. I suspect that Bath conveyed the body to a limestone cave on the River Murray, which was above the water line, and the abnormal flood this year has swept into the cave and carried the body into the main stream.

Indeed, in their second interview with Bath, the detectives told him that they were convinced this was where he had disposed of the body.

We are satisfied that the body had been buried in limestone country on the river bank and had been washed up by the big flood this year and also know it would be quite a simple matter for you to proceed on the Renmark Road on the other side of the river where the limestone deposits are at Murtho.

Bath neither rejected that theory, nor argued his innocence. He simply replied, "If you think I killed her, charge me."

22

ROAD TO TAREENA

If Bath killed Margaret at Renmark Railway Station, it can be assumed that he would have departed the area immediately. From sunrise on, travellers would have been arriving from all over the district and further afield to board the train for its scheduled departure for Adelaide at 7.30 am.

Bath told detectives that on leaving Renmark, he drove to the home of Bill Phillips, at Tareena Station over the border into New South Wales. Bath stated that he arrived that morning. However, Phillips testified that Bath arrived in his Packard car either as they were preparing lunch or during lunch. The journey from Renmark on Renmark Road to the Tareena property was forty miles.[21] On today's sealed road, the trip takes seventy minutes. On an unsealed road, as it

---

[21] Sixty-five kilometres

was in the early 1950s, it would have taken up to two hours. When questioned about the intervening hours, Bath claimed that the roads to Tareena Station were bad. Even so, there were between three to four missing hours for which he simply could not account.

Four hours was ample time for Bath to drive from Renmark Railway Station the twelve miles[22] to Murtho, dispose of the body in a limestone cave and then drive fifty-two miles[23] from Murtho to Tareena Station via Renmark.

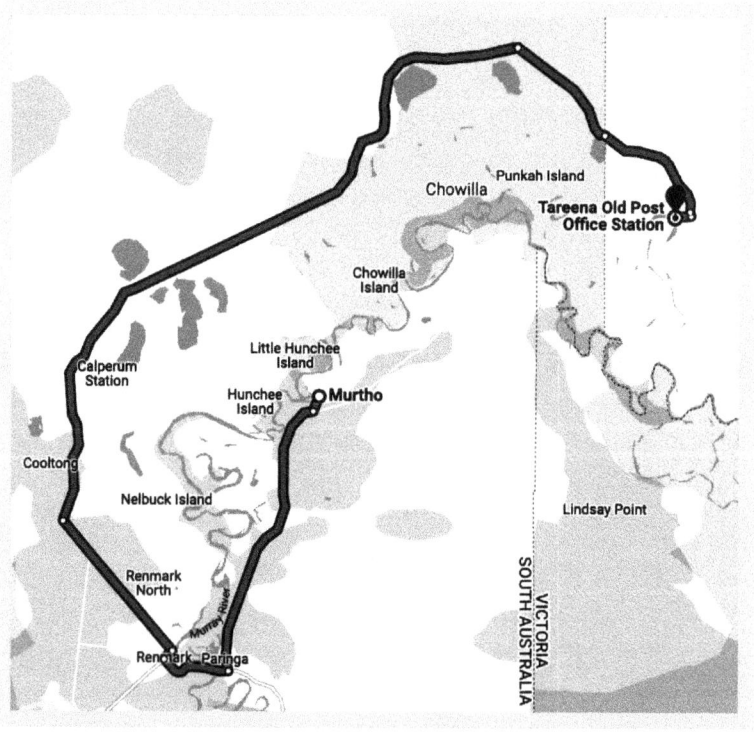

---

[22] Twenty kilometres
[23] Eighty-three kilometres

According to Bill Phillips, Bath appeared upset on arrival. "He said that Marg had had a nervous breakdown and left me. He told me that she had left him in Renmark."

The role of Russell Bath's brother Charlie in the death of Margaret Salter remains a mystery. But we do know that before shooting himself, Charlie Bath intimated that he was somehow involved in the case, proclaiming that if his brother was hanged, he would be hanged, too.

There are two possible scenarios: Charlie Bath was either present at Margaret's death or an accessory after the fact.

In his drunken interview with detectives, Charlie said that Russell had told him about Marg's disappearance, had insinuated that she was dead and that the body found in the river was hers. Charlie then advised Russell not to admit to anything, even if they threw tables and chairs at him.

If Charlie's account is true, he was not present when Margaret died. Therefore, he was likely implicated after the fact.

One could surmise that Russell Bath later coopted his bother to return with him to where he disposed of her body, to remove items of clothing, rings, teeth, etc., and to ensure that her body was never found.

Unfortunately, Charlie's suicide means that we will never know how he was involved.

23

PERSEVERE

In the end, the when, where and why are secondary to the question of how Bath got away with homicide. The answer to that question is simple - there was no way for the authorities to identify the petrified woman's body with certainty.

In the early 1950s, analysis of fingerprints and teeth were vital tools to identify victims of crime. But *The Petrified Woman* was devoid of both hands and teeth. In the late 20th century, DNA analysis transformed crime investigations, offering the means to identify perpetrators and victims. It has also revolutionised cold case investigations. Undoubtedly, DNA analysis could now resolve the petrified woman's identity.

When I first contacted Margaret Salter's granddaughter, Margaret Ellis, she was delighted about the possibility of

Pauper's Grave - West Terrace Cemetery

solving the mystery of her grandmother's disappearance and immediately agreed to a DNA test.

The result confirmed that she was Harry Salter's daughter and, therefore, the granddaughter of Margaret Salter (nee Wright), whose family had immigrated to Australia in the 1880s and settled in Adelaide.

In early 2018, I contacted the South Australian Police, alerting them to my research on the case and how I believed it could now be solved using Margaret Ellis's DNA. A week later, I received a call from a detective from the Major Crime Investigation Branch. He said he couldn't locate any records in the archives but expressed genuine interest in *The Petrified Woman* case.

I sent him copies of pathology and investigation reports and details of where the victim was buried. A few weeks later, he called to say the case had serious merit and that it fitted the aims of 'Operation Persevere', a recently announced mission to reinvestigate cases of long-term missing persons and unidentified human remains. And so began a constructive relationship with members of South Australia Police Major Crime Investigation Branch.

In May 2019, I flew from Sydney to Adelaide to film scenes for Final Rendezvous, an investigative documentary about a failed espionage case from the early 1960s. While there, I took the opportunity to visit West Terrace Cemetery, where *The Petrified Woman* was buried. I located the unmarked pauper's grave using a thumbnail map supplied by a cemetery official. Bereft of a gravestone, it was a dismal sight. Equally sad were the stories of the four other lost souls - two unnamed babies and two men - who shared the grave with her.

On my return to Sydney, I researched the backgrounds of those two men.

Carl Johnson (Johansen) was born in Uddevalla, Sweden, on March 7, 1891. He arrived at Port Adelaide in October 1914 and spent the rest of his life in South Australia working as an itinerant labourer. Johnson had come to the notice of authorities for various offences, including drunkenness, squatting in a disused house, and causing grievous bodily harm with a razor. He died in Royal Adelaide Hospital on October 15, 1951.

The other man interred with *The Petrified Woman* was Michael Joseph Connole. Born in Adelaide in 1871 to James and Mary Connole (nee Carmody), he began to suffer delusions at the age of twenty. Eight years later, in 1899, he was admitted to Parkside Asylum, where he lived for the next fifty-two years until his death on December 13, 1951.

Neither Connole or Johnson had married and there is no record of any direct living descendants.

In October 2021, I assisted Margaret Ellis with an application to the South Australia Attorney General for an Exhumation License to recover the remains of *The Petrified Woman's* body to allow formal identification using DNA testing. The application contained extensive background information about the case, the location of the grave and detailed histories of the two men with whom *The Petrified Woman* shared the grave.

We nominated a funeral director who had recently assisted a South Australian family in disinterring two relatives from a cemetery recently sold to a commercial company. The family feared the graveyard would one day be bulldozed. The South Australian government approved that application, and the exhumation and reinterment at another cemetery went smoothly. Margaret Ellis hoped for a similar positive outcome for *The Petrified Woman*.

Six months earlier, in May 2021, the Attorney-General of South Australia Vickie Chapman had approved an application to exhume the remains of the Somerton Man, an unidentified man found dead on Somerton Beach in December 1948.

The mystery surrounding the Somerton Man's death and identity became a global media sensation thanks mainly to the dogged research carried out by Adelaide University Professor Derek Abbott. The exhumation from Adelaide's

West Terrace Cemetery, the same cemetery where the Petrified Woman is buried, was privately funded but overseen by officers of South Australia's Major Crime Investigation Branch. DNA extracted from the remains is expected to identify the man.

However, months before the Somerton Man exhumation, Professor Abbott seconded Adelaide University's Forensics Lab to analyse a hair found on the mystery man's death mask, using DNA sequencing. From the results, Abbott and forensic genealogist Colleen Fitzpatrick found a DNA match in a genealogical database, then constructed an extended family tree until they found someone who fitted the description of Somerton Man.

In August 2022, Derek Abbott announced that the Somerton Man had been identified as Carl "Charles" Webb, an electrical engineer from Melbourne who had vanished from public records in April 1947.

The Somerton Man breakthrough made headlines worldwide, but also drew criticism, as the police analysis of DNA taken from the exhumed remains had not yet been completed.

Derek Abbott and I had corresponded many times over the previous fifteen years. I admired his painstaking work on the Somerton Man case and was aghast at the criticism and vitriol he received from many quarters during his investigation. Indeed, the case highlighted some of the difficulties private citizens face when they take on what has traditionally been a matter for the police and government forensic agencies.

Fearing that the Somerton Man controversy might impact *The Petrified Woman* case, I decided that Margaret Ellis's application for an exhumation needed to be lodged without media attention.

Unfortunately, political ructions within the South Australian State Government, followed by a state election, saw the exhumation application pass through the hands of three consecutive South Australian Attorneys-General in quick succession.

In 2022, Margaret Ellis telephoned me to say that the new Attorney-General had rejected her application, citing the complexity of multiple bodies buried in the same plot and West Terrace Cemetery's argument that it could not guarantee the grave's exact location, even though it's general position is known to with a metre or two.

There was also the issue of who would pay the costs. In a just world, the expense involved in solving a murder case is invariably borne by the state, not the victim's family.

While the original inquest exposed the limits of forensic science in the 1950s, there is no such excuse today. Even if the grave's exact location is in doubt it can be detected using modern technology. Indeed, exhumations are today carried out on historic battlefields with the aid of ground-penetrating radar. In 2006, the Australian Army and the United Kingdom Ministry of Defence commissioned a joint project to find Allied soldiers buried in pits near the village of Fromelles in France in 1916. Ground-penetrating radar was used to confirm the locations. Using a specialist team of forensic and investigative professionals, all the pits were opened, and the remains of 250 Australian and British soldiers were successfully exhumed and identified. The reinterment phase concluded in July 2010 when the Governor General of Australia, Quentin Bryce, His Royal Highness, The Prince of Wales Prince Charles,[24] government representatives, relatives and more than five thousand spectators watched as soldiers from the Australian and British Armies laid the final soldier to rest. The ceremony was televised worldwide as a fitting conclusion to several years of marvellous work.

By August 2022, Operation Persevere had successfully identified the remains of ten unidentified South Australians. At that time, the Minister for Police, Joe Szakacs, said that South Australia Police continue to pursue all avenues of enquiry until an individual is located.

"South Australia Police endeavour to give the families of missing persons answers as to why their loved one has disappeared," Minister Szakacs said.

Unfortunately, the case of *The Petrified Woman*, which is noted as 52/01 on the Operation Persevere list, remains in limbo. Hopefully, the evidence presented in this book will convince the South Australian Government to reconsider its position and allow her remains to be exhumed and finally identified.

---

[24] Now His Majesty King Charles III

24

AFTERWORD

There were many players in this story, and most were private citizens who left no trail for the researcher. But I was able to find details about a few.

Margaret Salter's son Harry Salter died in Adelaide in 2003, aged 93.

Gallipoli veteran and owner of Lindsay Point Station, Humphrey Kempe, authored two splendid books, The Astonished Earth and An Account of Connected Passages Participation. He died in Adelaide in 1986, aged 91.

With her reputation in tatters after a series of adulterous affairs and her relationship with murder suspect Russell Bath, Lucy Jessy Snook fled her home state of South Australia for good. She moved to the working-class suburb of Balmain in Sydney, New South Wales. Coincidentally, she settled less than a hundred metres from my grandparents' home, where my father and his sisters were born. Lucy Snook passed away in 1971.

Detective David Flint, who retrieved the body of *The Petrified Woman* and was a leading player in the investigation, lived to the grand age of 98. He died in Renmark on October 21, 2000.

Following the Coronial Inquest, Russell Rufus Bath drifted south and ended up in the Victorian township of Lake Bolac. He apparently married and fathered three children. He died in January, 30, 1982, aged 72, and buried at Nichols Point Cemetery in Mildura, Victoria.

Meanwhile, Margaret Salter, aka Mrs Margaret Bath, who went missing in April 1951, resides in an unmarked pauper's grave in Adelaide's West Terrace Cemetery. She is survived by her granddaughter, Margaret Ellis and grandson, Ted, and more than thirty other living descendants.

ILLUSTRATIONS

Detective David Flint - Greg Flint
Wood Engraving for *The Return of The Native* - Agnes Miller Parker.
Victim body sketch - South Australia Coronial documents
Lindsay Point Station - *The Astonished Earth* - Humphrey Kempe
The Fisherman - Linocut by Rex Wood (Manuscripts No:9, May 22, 1934)
Sheerer No 6, Wood Engraving by Myrtle Fasten
Wood Engraving for Alec Waugh's *"Most Women"*, by Lynd Ward
Woman and Child - State Library of NSW
Wire Bed - Helen Ogilvie
Wilkinsons Cliffs
Theft of Petrified Man - The Mail Adelaide 5 December 1953 page 4
Prelude to a Million Years -Wood Engraving Lynd Ward, 1933
Petrified Man Bondi - R. Wolfe Collection, State Library of NSW
Lucy Snook - Ancestry.com
Agnes Miller Parker - Wood Engraving for *"The Return of The Native"*
Wood Engraving for *Vertigo* 1937 - Lynd Ward
Wood Engraving for *"The Return of The Native"* - Agnes Miller Parker
Renmark Court House - Trove
Scraper Board (Circus) - D. J. Finley (Manuscripts No:9, May 22, 1934)
To the Hills - Elioth Gruner
Renmark Railway Station
Fractured Skull - South Australia Coroner
Pauper's Grave - West Terrace Cemetery
The Fisherman - Linocut by Rex Wood (Manuscripts No:9, May 22, 1934)

ACKNOWLEDGEMENTS

For their assistance on this project, I am indebted to Margaret Ellis, Merridy Kempe, Greg Flint, Stephen Scheding and South Australia Police Major Crime Investigation Branch.

A special thanks to my dear wife Sarah Staveley for her love, encouragement and superb editing and research skills.

BLACKWATTLE PRESS

Investigative True Crime Books

The Bogle-Chandler mystery is recognised as one of the most baffling cold cases in the annals of crime. Brilliant physicist Dr Gilbert Bogle and Mrs Margaret Chandler, the wife of his colleague, were found dead beside a picturesque river in Sydney, Australia. Investigators found no evidence to suggest how they had died. The police immediately suspected Geoffrey Chandler as the killer. But despite drawing on the expertise of police and forensic agencies around the world, the coroner was unable to determine how the victims met their fate. Author Peter Butt presents new evidence, which provides a solution to the mystery. This revised edition, features the explosive testimony of a previously unknown witness to the deaths - a testimony that should thrust the case back onto the coroner's desk.

In 1980, following the mysterious death of Australian merchant banker, Frank Nugan, his New York-born business partner, Michael Hand, brazenly ordered the destruction of the bank's records. Hand then disappeared from Sydney and hasn't been seen since. Among the ruins of the Nugan Hand global financial empire, investigators uncovered astonishing evidence of gunrunning, money laundering for drug traffickers and connections to the CIA. When the FBI and a Royal Commission failed to join the dots, those intimately involved with the case suspected a cover up. Brimming with chilling new evidence and powerful testimonies, Author Peter Butt cracks open the sensational Nugan Hand story and goes on the hunt for the world's most elusive corporate fugitive…

It is 1743, and Great Britain's coffers are overflowing with the profits of Caribbean sugar. But when a spat between two London schoolboys turns deadly, the simmering contempt between London's powerful sugar merchants and the Establishment is laid bare. As the ring of Newgate Prison's execution bell draws menacingly closer, a desperate family seeks salvation from the King. Author Sarah Staveley evokes an era and its people as she interrogates in forensic detail a sensational criminal case and uncovers its unexpected, heart-wrenching aftermath.

Purchase Direct From
Blackwattle Press

"The Mystery of the Century!"

DR BOGLE & MRS CHANDLER
The Confession

PETER BUTT

DR BOGLE MRS CHANDLER

The Confession

PETER BUTT

BLACKWATTLE PRESS

DOUGLAS STEWART PRIZE JUDGES' COMMENTS

The 'Bogle and Chandler' case was one of the most famous unsolved mysteries in Australia, involving an eminent scientist and the wife of one of his colleagues found dead and nearly naked on the banks of the Lane Cove River in Sydney. Peter Butt has taken up the challenge of solving the mystery in this 'true crime' narrative, as he uncovers the original investigation, interviews all the participants and comes up with an unexpected—and convincing—new theory. It's a theory that moves the book from 'whodunnit' into 'environmental thriller' without ever losing its command of the evidence or narrative style.

Peter Butt has marshalled a vast array of information and interviewed dozens of people, pulling together an involving, fast-paced story with the significant contemporary themes of gender and the environment. The writing is clear and engaging, even when he presents detailed scientific material; the characterisations are compelling, the culture of the period is well observed and the exploration of how the Bogle and Chandler deaths happened is fascinating. The opening out of the story into a social and environmental context makes this a valuable contribution to both 'true crime' and environmental literature.

1
New Year's Day

With its siren wailing, the NSW police-issue Studebaker Lark pulled out across the Pacific Highway against a red light. Working the morning shift on New Year's Day in Sydney, Sergeant Arthur Andrews and Senior Constable Nicholls had drawn the short straw. It was just after 10 am and unlike their colleagues, who were likely still sleeping off their celebratory excesses, their job was to clean up the worst of what the nascent hours of 1963 could muster.

Their vehicle sped down Millwood Avenue, past lifeless brick bungalows, around a long sweeping bend, until the Lane Cove River came into view. Beside Fullers Bridge, two grim-faced teenage boys waved the car around the corner to the entrance of the riverside track.

The youths led the way. On the left, towering eucalypts clung to sandstone outcrops. To the right, she-oaks whistled in the gentle summer breeze and contorted mangroves crowded the muddy riverbed. Through the discord of vegetation, the river was dark and stagnant.

Like most Chatswood policemen, Andrews had routinely patrolled the secluded track looking for rubbish dumpers and voyeurs who stalked young lovers parked in their cars. This callout, however, sounded far more serious.

Eighty metres along the track, they came upon a man in a dark-grey suit, lying face down on a grassy verge by the riverbank. Nicholls ushered the boys back as Andrews knelt and gingerly lifted the man's wrist. His skin was cold to touch. There was no pulse. The man's face, turned side-on, had a blue-purple hue. A small amount of bloodstained mucus was evident below his right nostril. A patch of vomit lay nearby.

Fifteen-year-old Michael McCormick said he had taken the bush track at around 8.30 am to meet a friend at the Chatswood Golf Links where they planned to collect golf balls. It was then that he first saw the man lying there. He thought the fellow was merely drunk and had passed out. An hour or so later, McCormick and his friend, Denis Wheway, returned along the track. The man hadn't moved and his lips and face had turned purple. They went for help, stopping a moment on the bridge to look for fish. The proprietor of the park kiosk, Geoffrey Little, accompanied the boys back to where they had found the man. Mr Little had seen plenty of dead men in the war and this fellow certainly looked dead. He hurried back to his kiosk and called the police.

As Andrews walked around the body he noticed something peculiar about the clothing. The suit was draped over the man, giving the impression that he was dressed. He peeled off the suit coat to find something equally curious—a rectangular portion of dirty-brown carpet lying on top of his shirt. Andrews then lifted the trousers. The dead man was naked from the waist down except for his socks and muddied shoes.

Andrews turned the body onto its side. It was semi-rigid. He looked for signs of injury, but there was nothing to suggest he had met with a violent death.

Senior Constable Nicholls radioed for assistance. Ten minutes later, three more policemen arrived, including Detective Sergeant Henry Parsons, who managed a large team of detectives.

Parsons inspected the wallet taken from the dead man's coat pocket and then returned to Chatswood Police Station to make enquiries, leaving instructions with his men to search the area for evidence.

1 New Year's Day

Dr Bogle beside the Lane Cove River [re-enactment]

If the state of the man's clothing wasn't puzzling enough, the riverside location was to deliver another surprise. Searching downstream, in the direction of the golf links, a constable came across an unusual array of flattened-out beer cartons on the muddy riverbed.

On closer inspection, he noticed a human leg protruding slightly from beneath the cardboard.

'There's another one down here!' he yelled.

Andrews lifted the cartons, revealing the lifeless face of a pretty woman in her late twenties. Her clothing was in disarray. Both her rose-patterned, white dress and half-slip were gathered up, exposing the lower half of her body. The shoulder straps of the dress were down at her waist, along with her bra. Her slip, knees and bare feet were stained with black mud. At her feet lay a pair of men's jockey style underpants, wet and stained with excreta. It was an incongruous sight—a pretty woman in a white party dress amongst all that mud, reeking of faeces.

Mrs Chandler [re-enactment]

On receipt of a radio message about the find, Parsons returned to the crime scene, slid down the grass-covered bank and lifted the victim's hand to check for a pulse. There was none.

'Still warm', he half-whispered.

Again, there were no obvious external signs to suggest how the victim had died. Strangely, there was nothing to identify the woman— no handbag or purse. She wore a simple wedding ring, but there was no inscription.

1 New Year's Day

Parsons pondered the crime scene: two bodies less than 18 metres apart, a male on the grassy bank, a female on the exposed riverbed, both half naked and strangely covered, but no signs of violence.

A detective radioed the details to Criminal Investigation Branch (CIB) headquarters in the city. Across town, the newsrooms of the major dailies also picked up the transmission. The Daily Mirror's Bill Jenkings was first at the scene. He reported:

The first thing that struck me as the photographer and I trekked down through the bush to the river was the overpowering stench of death. I could smell and see human excreta and vomit. The stifling morning heat seemed to magnify the putrid odour.[1]

While the previous evening had been cool, it was turning out to be a typically warm and steamy Sydney New Year's Day. But the vagaries of the weather were secondary for the detectives and uniformed policemen who were plodding through black, stinking mud and a tangle of mangroves searching for evidence on the riverbed. They had what appeared to be a double murder on their hands, and the tide was coming in fast.

Detective Sergeant Parsons and Constable Turner drove to Turramurra, a quiet, relatively new North Shore suburb about twenty minutes from Fullers Bridge. At the end of an unmade path shaded by gumtrees they came to a fashionable 1950s brick home. Mrs Vivienne Bogle appeared at the door holding a baby in her arms.

With her four children and two relatives present, Parsons handed Mrs Bogle a wallet. It was in the pocket of a man, he said, found deceased beside the Lane Cove River. Papers inside the wallet bore the name Dr Gilbert Stanley Bogle—a physicist with the CSIRO, the Commonwealth Scientific and Industrial Research Organisation.

Fighting back tears, she said he had left home at nine o'clock the previous evening to attend a New Year's Eve party at the home of a CSIRO colleague. At 5 am, she awoke to attend to her crying baby and became concerned that he had not returned home.

At 6.45 am, she telephoned the party hosts, Ken and Ruth Nash. Mrs

Nash had said not to worry. It was a very late party and he hadn't long left. As the hours passed, she had become increasingly concerned and telephoned the police to see if he'd been in a car accident.

Parsons said that it wasn't possible at this stage to determine what had happened to her husband. What he had to say next was lodged in his throat; Vivienne Bogle was obviously an upright woman. He explained that there was another person found nearby and that she was also deceased.

From Parson's description of the woman, Mrs Bogle couldn't fathom who she was, let alone what she was doing with her husband.

Leaving the grief-stricken family, the detectives had little to go on, other than the address of the New Year's Eve party that Dr Bogle had attended. Fifteen minutes later, they walked up the path of a well-maintained liver-brick bungalow in Waratah Street, Chatswood.

A short, nuggetty man with the creased face of a heavy smoker answered the door. Ken Nash confirmed that he and his wife had presided over a party and that Dr Gilbert Bogle was one of about twenty invited guests who had attended.

Ruth Nash, a tall, attractive woman in her forties, appeared from the kitchen as her husband ushered the detectives into a sitting room, still in disarray from the party.

Parsons explained that Dr Bogle had been found dead at the Lane Cove River. He asked the shocked hosts if a female wearing a rose-patterned dress had also attended the party. Ruth Nash glanced at her husband. There had been a guest wearing a white summer frock with roses, she said. Her name was Mrs Margaret Chandler.

Ken Nash recalled that Mrs Chandler had arrived at the party around 10.30 pm with her husband Geoffrey, a fellow CSIRO colleague, and that she had left the party at about the same time as Dr Bogle, unaccompanied by her husband.

1 New Year's Day

A raven's haunting cry echoed across the Lane Cove River valley as Parsons and Turner returned to the crime scene. In the dusty parking area beside Fullers Bridge, police officers were inspecting an old khaki-coloured Ford Prefect. On the rear seat, they found a leather-covered case containing a clarinet and a surrealist Picasso-style sketch depicting a two-faced head and an assortment of severed limbs. Above the steering wheel, tucked behind the sun-visor, they found the key to the vehicle. A registration check determined that it was Dr Bogle's car.

Meanwhile, sightseers had gathered on the bridge, trying to catch a glimpse of the police activity downstream where Scientific Investigation Branch detectives were now searching the area for evidence.

On the exposed riverbed below Dr Bogle's body, Scientific Detective George Lindsay photographed a pair of ladies' panties, a man's belt, and a pair of brown ladies' court shoes. The items of clothing were spread out in a distinct line running parallel to the riverbank.

Lindsay's boss, Detective Sergeant Alan Clarke, ordered a couple of luckless policemen to collect human excreta both from the riverbed and the riverbank near Dr Bogle's body. Two police divers conferred with Clarke. They had scrutinised the murky river, they said, but it offered too little visibility to search for evidence.

At 2 pm, the Government Medical Officer, Dr Brighton, arrived and examined both bodies. Pronouncing life extinct, he couldn't determine how either victim had died. Detectives then lifted Mrs Chandler's body from the riverbed and placed it face down onto newspapers spread across the sandy track.

Four decades on, George Lindsay recalled the mysterious state of both victims' bodies:

> My main job was to search for bullet holes or knife marks, or anything like that, to determine if they'd been assaulted in some way. There were no marks of any distinction. I had no suspicions how they died. They were just two young bodies. We couldn't work out the cause of death.[2]

According to the *Mirror's* crime reporter Bill Jenkings, everyone was eager to leave the site: 'Everyone's guts were churning from the foul smell ... the vapours of Death', he presumed.

As a mortuary van headed for the City Morgue, a large dog named Fritz breached the crime scene barricade, wandered along the riverbank, then bounded down onto the mudflats, oblivious to the drama that had just unfolded.

So began one of the longest homicide and forensic investigations in New South Wales' history. The lives of the victims and everyone associated with them would soon come under intense police scrutiny. The mystery surrounding the deaths would spark a fierce newspaper war, challenge conservative society, split families, ruin careers, cause mental breakdowns and suicides and drive some people out of the country for good.

Little did anyone realise that a witness to the deaths was still present in the vicinity—a witness whose own story was intimately entwined with the fate of the victims.

2.

Alibi

Thud. Thud. Thud.

At one o'clock that afternoon an insistent banging reverberated through a modest, timber-clad Croydon Park cottage. A tall redheaded man with an unkempt beard dragged himself from his bed, wandered into the room opposite and picked up a crying nine-month-old boy from his cot. Opening the front door, he squinted in the bright sun, trying to make out the silhouetted figures wearing hats in front of him. They looked like detectives, he thought.

'Geoffrey Chandler?' said one of the detectives.

'Yes,' said Chandler hesitantly, as a second child appeared from down the hall and held onto his leg.

'What time is it?' he half-grumbled.

'Is your wife home?'

'No.'

At 3 pm, the Burwood detectives delivered Chandler and his two children to Chatswood Police Station. Constable Taylor took the boys into her care as a detective ushered Chandler along a corridor. He had no idea what this was all about. He could only imagine that something had happened to his wife. Detective-Sergeant Parsons looked up from a newspaper as Chandler entered his office. Parsons motioned for him to take a seat but offered nothing in the way of pleasantries:

'Is your wife's name Margaret Olive Chandler?' he said flatly.

'Yes,' Chandler replied.

'Can you tell me where your wife is?'

'I have no idea where she is.'

Parsons slid the afternoon edition of the *Daily Mirror* across the desk and pointed to a front-page headline: 'Scientist, Woman in Death Mystery'.

The newspaper named Dr Gilbert Bogle and Mrs Margaret Chandler as the victims. His own name appeared as the woman's husband, misspelled 'Jeffrey' Chandler, an experimental officer of the Division of Radio Physics, CSIRO.

In 2005, Geoffrey Chandler recalled Parsons' calculating method:

> By this time the newspaper had an edition out with some great splurge on the front page. He showed that to me quite sort of cold-bloodedly to gauge my reaction, I guess. I was very tired from not having much sleep the night before. It was quite clear that their first and foremost thought was that I was responsible for Margaret's death.[3]

Parsons' intuitive, penetrating questioning had delivered confessions from scores of men and women sitting in that same chair. Many had received life sentences.

Parsons waited patiently for a reaction to the newspaper report. Finally, Chandler placed the paper on the desk, removed a cigarette from a pack in his shirt pocket and lit it. Strangely, he showed no emotion at the news of his wife's death.

Parsons asked Chandler about his and Margaret's relationship with the physicist, Dr Bogle.

'Gib' Bogle, he said, had been a colleague of his at the CSIRO for a number of years. They worked in different departments on different floors. Occasionally, they would pass each other in the corridor and say hello. He said that Margaret first met Bogle ten days earlier at a

2. Alibi

CSIRO Christmas party held at a Radio Astronomy facility at Murray-bank. They had spent some time talking. Later that night, they had all gone back to the home of Ken and Ruth Nash for drinks. At Dr Bogle's suggestion, Nash had invited them to their New Year's Eve party.

Geoffrey Chandler

Asked if his wife had further contact with Dr Bogle after the Christmas party, Chandler said with certainty that the next time they met was at the New Year's Eve party. Parsons also questioned Chandler on his and Margaret's movements before, during and after the party.

The previous night, he said, they had left their two children at Margaret's parents' home in Granville and arrived at the party in Chatswood around 10.30 pm.

Dressed in slacks, shirtsleeves and sandals, Chandler said that he had felt uncomfortable; the other men were wearing suits and ties. Margaret looked pretty in a summer, rose-patterned dress but the other women were more conservatively dressed.

Chandler said that at around 11.30 pm he told Margaret that he was going to buy cigarettes and then left the party on his own. Just before midnight he arrived at another party in Phoebe Street, Balmain. The host, Ken Buckley, a controversial left-wing Professor of Economics at Sydney University, was renowned for his wild parties.

Chandler found Buckley's bash to be the antithesis of the effete Chatswood soirée. In the garden, he eased up to Pamela Logan, a twenty-one-year-old Sydney University Psychology Department secretary.

At 1.30 am, Chandler and Logan left the Balmain party, driving in separate cars to Logan's rented room in Darlington. Half an hour later, Chandler said, he left Miss Logan and returned to the Chatswood party, arriving as supper was being served. An hour or so later, at around 4 am, he left the party on his own, for a second time.

'Did you have an argument with your wife?' asked Parsons.

'No. My wife was to go with Dr Bogle by arrangement with my wife.'

'What do you mean by an arrangement?'

'By this I mean they both wished to go home together and I felt no objection towards this. They were attracted to each other.'

'Attracted to each other? Has your wife previously gone home from parties by arrangement with yourself?'

'No, she hadn't done this before, but I had no objection to her going home with him and having intercourse with him if she wanted it, and he wanted to have it with her.'

The explanation confounded Parsons. Chandler then recalled his parting words to Dr Bogle:

'I said to Gib, "Tell Margaret not to worry. I'll pick up the children from her parents' home".'

Chandler explained that on leaving the party he had driven across

2. Alibi

the Harbour Bridge and returned to Pamela Logan's bedsitter. A little later they set off together to his wife's parents' home in Granville to pick up his children.

Parsons scribbled on his note pad: *Chandler takes girlfriend to in-law's house!*

Chandler didn't appear to be hiding anything. On the contrary, he was open about his affair with Pamela Logan. He had also admitted leaving his wife at the Chatswood party, not once but twice. The second time was just after 4 am—about an hour before his wife and Dr Bogle had met their deaths.

To test Chandler's extraordinary alibi, Parsons and Constable Turner drove to Darlington on the south side of the city.

At 4.20 pm, a striking, blonde-haired young woman came to her door. Even in a housedress and wearing a ponytail, Pamela Logan projected sophistication beyond her twenty-one years. Little did she realise that the doorbell had sounded the beginning of a bruising heavyweight bout that would batter her previously untarnished public reputation.

After presenting his identification, Parsons asked if Geoffrey Chandler had been in her company the previous evening and earlier that morning. Logan confirmed that she had been with Chandler and questioned why they wanted to know.

Parsons said that Chandler had told them 'certain things' and suggested that she could confirm them.

Logan reluctantly invited the detectives in. Seated at the kitchen table, she told them that Geoffrey had arrived at the Balmain party about midnight and that they left together about 1.30 am, driving in their own cars to her Darlington bed-sitter. Half an hour later, Chandler had departed and she went to bed. At about 4.30 am she had been woken by a knock at the door. Chandler had returned. She was annoyed, she said, but he somehow cajoled her to go with him to pick up his children from his in-laws' home at Granville. As she dressed, she noticed that it was 5 am on her bedside clock.

On the journey to Granville, Chandler told her that he had deliberately arranged for Dr Bogle to take his wife home and expected them to have intercourse.

As they approached Granville, Chandler dropped her off on Parramatta Road while he went to collect two-year-old Gareth and nine-month-old Sean. On the return journey, their car ran out of petrol. Three young men offered assistance and they finally arrived back at her home about 6 am, where Chandler and the children remained until 10 am.

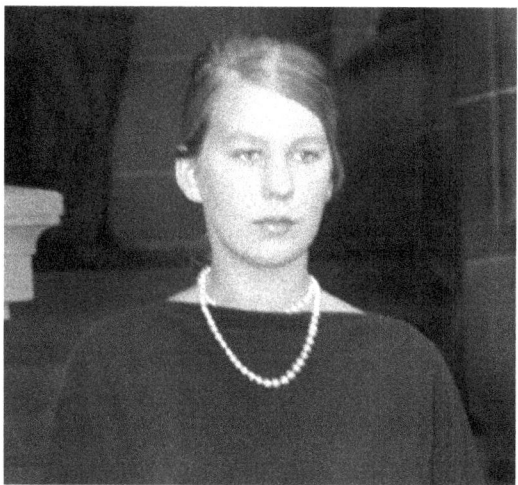

Pamela Logan

As incredible as Logan's account sounded, it neatly matched Geoffrey Chandler's version of events.

Logan pressed Parsons to explain what had happened, insisting that she was not about to answer any further questions without a lawyer. Using a powerful tactic designed to terrify young people and goad them into cooperating, Parsons asked where her parents were. They lived in Sydney, she said, but refused to divulge their address.

2. Alibi

Parsons asked if she knew Geoffrey Chandler was married and whether or not Mrs Chandler knew about her. Logan demanded to know 'what that had to do with anything.'

Parsons contemplated the young, frightened woman a moment. He then leaned forward and said bluntly, 'Do you know that Mrs Chandler and a Dr Gilbert Bogle were found dead this morning?'

Pamela Logan immediately burst into tears. There appeared to be nothing artificial about her reaction.

¶

Parsons returned to Chatswood Police Station. At 9 pm, Detective Inspector Watson, whom the CIB had sent over to take charge of the investigation, reinterviewed Chandler, both for the benefit of obtaining a signed, typewritten statement and to test his consistency.

Watson quizzed him about his relationship with his wife. Chandler claimed that he and Margaret had a happy marriage. But he also had no problem with her taking a lover, as he believed it would be 'transitory'. To prove his point, he said Margaret had previously had an affair with a friend of his, both with his knowledge and approval. He claimed that it had no negative impact at all on his marriage and only enhanced it. Even for the world-weary detectives, such a liberal attitude was incomprehensible.

As the grilling continued, Chandler sensed that he remained their prime suspect:

> They were convinced that I was the killer, and they did everything they could to sort of prove that that was the case. They didn't use any overt physical force, but there was an awful lot of covert intimidation, like the big burly copper with a gun on his belt standing alongside my ear. I just went into a state of tight internal control where the purpose was to survive this scene with the police.[4]

The interview ended at 2 am, thirteen arduous hours after Chandler had opened his door to the detectives. At this stage, there was nothing to connect him to the riverside deaths of his wife and Dr Gilbert Bogle. Yet his extraordinarily cool, unemotional testimony did nothing to allay suspicions. If Geoffrey Chandler was a double-murderer, he was certainly a clever one.

A morsel of sweetness is all that stands between life and death...

A CONSEQUENCE OF CAKE

Sarah Staveley

A CONSEQUENCE OF CAKE

by

Sarah Staveley

Based on actual events

Part One

1. Eleven Apostles

Monday, September 26, 1743, had been an unseasonably warm market day at Smithfield. As evening fell on the City of London, a coach wound its way carefully from London Bridge through streets still clogged with drovers, cattle and squealing hogs. The sole occupant of the coach, ruddy-faced Beeston Long, held a rose-scented handkerchief to his nose in an effort to disguise the pervasive odour of livestock.

Eventually, the carriage entered Leadenhall Street and pulled up outside a residence near the stone-arched doors of East India House.[2] It was from this building, belonging to Long's brother-in-law and business partner Roger Drake, that the two men ran the Drake and Long Company, their highly successful enterprise as sugar factors and colonial agents.

Long was bathed in perspiration by the time he reached his third-floor rooms. Having established that no one else was about, he removed his frock-coat and cocked hat, placed both items on a coat stand, then mopped his forehead and neck with a fresh handkerchief. Sitting down at his leather-top desk, he pulled a silver tray towards him and retrieved a large bundle of correspondence, all addressed to his attention.

As he scanned the pile, a letter, marked as urgent, piqued Long's interest. It bore the seal of Martin Clare, headmaster of the Academy in Soho Square, where several of his wards boarded.

The headmaster's note had been crafted to inform rather than to alarm. Clare advised that an incident had occurred at the Academy early that afternoon. One of their wards, Thomas Waite Ricketts, had sustained a small wound, which was not deemed serious.

Long searched through the remaining letters on his tray, then scoured Drake's desk. Finding nothing more from Martin Clare, he hurried downstairs to check with the footman, who confirmed that no further correspondence had arrived from the Soho Academy.

Beeston Long was a gentleman of thirty-two and well on his way to building a considerable fortune in the City of London.[3] He possessed in abundance the qualities required of a successful merchant. He was clever, personable, meticulous, driven, and astute in assessing risk. Accordingly, his sleep that night was made uneasy by a creeping concern for the welfare of young Ricketts.

Soho Square lay four miles west of Leadenhall Street. Its neat five-storey terraces of red brick and white sash windows were the product of London's frenetic construction activity after the Great Fire, prior to which it had been agricultural lands known as Soho Fields. The new Square featured at its centre a statue of the restored Stuart King, Charles II,[4] and for a time, England's elite had flocked there. The 1st Duke of Monmouth had even commissioned Christopher Wren to design his Monmouth House mansion at its southern end.[5] But soon enough, newer, grander homes in Mayfair and Belgravia had lured the upper classes westward. Though still a prestigious address in 1743, Soho Square was well past its fashionable residential heyday. It was now occupied by a mixture of residential and business tenants, the rowdiest of whom were undoubtedly housed within the walls of Mr Clare's Academy at number 8. The incident in question occurred earlier that afternoon in the second-floor dining room. Midday dinner had been cleared away and a short rest time instituted before the resumption of classes. The dining room also doubled as a dormitory, and young Samuel Malcher sat reading a book, only lifting his head occasionally to whinge about the general stuffiness of the room and the silly rule that prevented him from opening the windows.

In the far corner of the room, an older boy, William Chetwynd, had been busy stowing away books, inkpots and writing utensils into the small drawers of his walnut-wood writing desk. Very carefully, he had then dropped the desk's fall front into full extension, and onto it laid a cake that he retrieved from a wooden box on the floor. Taking a few steps back, he admired the temptation before him. It was a fine example of a Simnel cake - a large, aromatic fruitcake covered with a layer of scorched marzipan, on top of which were perched eleven marble-sized marzipan balls evenly distributed around its outer edge. It had been baked to the traditional English recipe: muscovado sugar, cherries, citrus peel, sultanas, flour, and mixed spice, all stirred together, with sweet almond marzipan melted through its middle. It was enough to make any schoolboy salivate in anticipation.

Samuel Malcher placed his book down and dashed over to inspect the cake. If he had half hoped his interest would be rewarded with the offer of a piece, he was disappointed. He simply received a short oration from William Chetwynd on the significance of the cake's decoration. The eleven balls on top were said to represent Jesus' apostles, with the pointed exclusion of Judas, who, but for his betrayal of Jesus, would have made the twelfth.

Malcher rolled his eyes, explaining that he knew about Simnel cake, but wondered why it had been baked and delivered three days before Michaelmas.[6] He was fairly certain that Simnel was a cake for Lent.

As Chetwynd turned to respond, he was interrupted by the abrupt, prancing arrival of Thomas Ricketts into the room. The tall, gangly, high-spirited lad loudly announced to William Chetwynd that it was time for their fencing class. But Ricketts' eagerness for fencing swiftly evaporated on seeing and smelling William Chetwynd's magnificent marzipan confection.

The Bible warns, "*For the love of money is the root of all evil: which while some coveted after, they have erred from the faith, and pierced themselves through with many sorrows.*"[7]

Sadly, the scriptures have nothing to say about the consequences of the love of cake, which is a pity. Had they done so, perhaps the fracas that was about to ensue may have been averted.

2. The Bucket

Before dawn the following day, Beeston Long dispatched a note to the Garlick Hill home of his friend, Peter St Hill. The eminent physician regularly tended to Long's wards when ill or injured.

Indicating that the matter was urgent, Long requested that they meet at the Soho Academy at ten o'clock.[8] However, Long had not anticipated terror in the streets. A horned bullock had run amok from Smithfield that morning, making the journey from Leadenhall Street one of frustrating delays and diversions.[9] Consequently, it was well after ten when Long alighted his carriage outside the green door of number 8 Soho Square. Next to it, a gleaming brass plaque declared this to be Mr Clare's Soho Academy.

Martin Clare was only in his twenties when he founded his Academy at 1 Soho Square in 1717. His aim was to *'fit young men for trade and business.'* He quickly found a clientele amongst wealthy and upper-class parents. Indeed, the aristocracy of England was awash with boys of lowly birth order who stood to inherit little other than a respected surname. Such boys were obliged to make their own way in the world.

Under the roof of the Soho Academy, Clare brought together boys of the upper and middling orders and prepared them to become Britain's next generation of merchants. Fortunately for Clare, this was a boom time for merchants, and their wealth was fast rivalling the inherited wealth of many a British nobleman.

Early in the Academy's history, Clare wrote and published *Youth's Introduction to Trade and Business*, a textbook for aspiring merchants that proved to be a classic and his calling card.[10] Clare was as brilliant an entrepreneur as he was an educator. His curriculum cleverly combined trade-related classes in mathematics, geography, reason, and scientific method, with more traditional classes in French, drama, morality, and fencing, all of it underpinned by a healthy dose of Church of England Christianity. The Soho Academy was a fashionable success, so much so that by 1725 Clare needed to lease larger premises, which he conveniently found across the Square at number 8.[11]

Clare's maidservant, Hannah, greeted Beeston Long at the door. Hannah was generally cheery and engaging, even comical on occasion, but she was none of those things this morning. She was duly courteous to Long but quickly disappeared up the uncarpeted wooden staircase to the first floor, leaving him standing alone in the entrance hall. Above him, Long could hear booming voices, the dragging of furniture on floorboards, and then a loud bang followed by laughter. He looked up at the ceiling and smiled. His own classrooms at Eton had sounded much the same.

Minutes later, Hannah reappeared at the top of the first-floor landing, accompanied by her master. Martin Clare nodded to Long, acknowledging him. The headmaster was renowned for his youthful geniality and a glorious enthusiasm that seemed to belie his fifty-five years. But Long was startled by the visible alteration in Clare. He appeared tired, frail, and sombre, his forehead imprinted with a frown. Clearly, all was not well. As he descended the stairs, Clare held the handrail and, on occasion, needed to be steadied by Hannah.

Clare took the younger man's hand in greeting but said nothing. Instead, he guided Long back up the stairs and into a small makeshift sickroom.

On a bed in the middle of the room lay a quietly moaning Thomas Ricketts, his cheeks wet with tears, his forehead soaked in sweat, his belly grossly distended. Foul, blood-stained bandages lay in a bucket next to the bed. Long's friend, Peter St Hill, was examining a knife wound to Ricketts' stomach, observed by the Academy's regular physician, Peter Macculloch, and two visiting physicians, John Shipton and David Middleton.[12]

With Clare's manservant assisting, St Hill redressed the wound. He then rose slowly and a little stiffly, his nod of acquiescence to all in the room, though imperceptible to the patient, sufficient to indicate to Beeston Long that the situation was grave.

Long was floored. His first instinct was to prise an account of the incident directly from his ward while there was still time. St Hill agreed that a short conversation with Ricketts would be possible.

Long pulled up a seat beside the bed, leaned in closely and wiped the patient's forehead dry with his clean linen handkerchief. Despite his condition, Thomas was coherent and able to explain the previous afternoon's events.

Twenty minutes later, Long withdrew from the room to speak with the schoolmaster.

Martin Clare offered an embarrassed apology. He explained his understanding of what had transpired the previous afternoon and his horror on learning that

Ricketts' condition had deteriorated drastically during the night.

Long tempered his response out of respect for Clare but was adamant on one thing; he wanted a meeting with the perpetrator. But this was a request Martin Clare could not fulfil. Earlier that morning, the boy, shaken by all that had happened, had panicked and fled from the Academy to the home of his aunt and uncle in Upper Grosvenor Street, Mayfair. Clare had just received word that the boy was in deep distress and keenly awaited news of Ricketts.

Comforted that St Hill had agreed to revisit the patient the following morning, Long decided against compounding the headmaster's vexation with further demands. Instead, he took his leave of the Academy and returned to Leadenhall Street to deliver the shocking news to his business partner, Roger Drake.

The following morning, Peter St Hill returned to the Academy to find a weary Macculloch tending faithfully to Thomas Ricketts' bandages and mopping up the sweat that seeped continually from his body. Throughout the night, the patient had flailed about on his bed, his agony intensifying. St Hill inspected Ricketts' belly. It was less swollen, but the pain he was experiencing in the upper area of the swelling had intensified. His pulse was very fast, and his blood pressure dangerously low. He hiccupped continually and vomited bile and other stinking matter. While Macculloch and St Hill were eminent in their fields, they had no remedy for what ailed Thomas Ricketts. All they could do now was pray.

A little after six on Thursday morning, September 29, Thomas Ricketts fell unconscious. Macculloch woke the headmaster, who came and held his pupil's hand for almost an hour, praying for him and showing a father's tenderness until it was evident that the lad was no longer breathing.

Martin Clare's whole body shook, and his teeth chattered as he sat at his desk and wrote two notes, one addressed to Leadenhall Street in the City and the other to 19 Upper Grosvenor Street in Mayfair.

His wife brought him tea and urged him to eat and rest, but Clare was neither hungry nor thirsty and had no intention of stopping. He spent the remainder of the day on a frenzied mission, writing to the parents and guardians of his pupils, informing them of what had taken place and assuring them that their sons and wards remained safe under the Academy's care. Then, to ensure this was the case, he instructed his deputy headmaster, Cuthbert Barwis, to confiscate all clasp knives, scissors, compasses, and experimental equipment. He also insisted that fencing swords be locked away, and the downstairs kitchen made permanently out of bounds to all pupils, with immediate effect.

Martin Clare realised that he had allowed himself to become distracted from the daily operation of his Academy, his life's great work. Now an innocent young man had paid the price for that distraction. A scandal was inevitable, and the reputation of the Soho Academy was almost certainly ruined. He did not expect to be forgiven and could not forgive himself.

THE **TRUE STORY** OF THE NUGAN HAND BANK SCANDAL

MERCHANTS OF MENACE

PETER BUTT

THE TRUE STORY OF THE NUGAN HAND BANK SCANDAL

MERCHANTS OF MENACE

PETER BUTT

BLACKWATTLE PRESS
3P

PROLOGUE

HEALTHY, WEALTY GUYS

On 15 October 1979, a mysterious procession of late-model Mercedes Benz motored slowly through Sydney past the Opera House, up Macquarie Street, around Hyde Park and along William Street, taking in the atmosphere of the city. Anyone who caught sight of the ostentatious procession may have pondered the identity of the occupants. Perhaps they were foreign dignitaries, maybe celebrities. In fact, they were international representatives of a little-known merchant bank, Nugan Hand, which in a mere matter of months would make headline news across Australia and around the world.

The purring silver and gold chariots turned left into Darlinghurst Road and entered Kings Cross, the so-called 'glittering mile of dreams', which, curiously, measured a half mile at most. Below garish neon signs, strip-show spruikers were pacing bloodstained pavements, circling potential customers like swamp mosquitoes sniffing out a feast. In nearby bars, battalions of suburban warriors were fomenting war against bouncers or anyone else who might cross their path. After a bit of blood and chunder, they would likely stumble into the narrow alleyways where sweaty pimps offered up an assortment of their glazed-eye, scantily clad doxies. What had started in the 1900s with sly-groggers, fortune tellers and goodtime girls was now Australia's heartland of vice and crime, in which drugs and sex were the major currencies.

The fleet cruised by the famed flesh palaces, the Pink Pussy Cat and Les Girls nightclubs, and slowed reverentially at the next bend, opposite the Bourbon & Beefsteak Bar and Restaurant.

'This is where it all began,' they had been told over and over. 'At the Bourbon; that's where Mike and Frank first met!'

*

The tour terminated at the elegant Gazebo Hotel, the tallest building in Kings Cross, where the merchant bankers had already been gathered for a company talkfest for the past three days.

In an anteroom, Michael Hand gathered his thoughts. He was pushing thirty-eight and the mirror in front of him didn't lie. Since leaving the military, he'd worked hard to maintain his muscled physique at the gym. He'd even installed a treadmill in his Hong Kong office, but all the long business lunches, the international travel and the steroids had taken their toll and he'd gone to mush. Still, a Singapore tailor had crafted a suit that concealed his expanding girth and, when all was said and done, with his thick, dark brown hair and manicured nails, he still looked 'suave de boney', as his army buddy Douglas A Sapper III used to say.

Michael entered the conference room. The two dozen delegates took their seats as he walked over to the lectern and tapped the microphone. The large banner behind him, adorned with the flags of thirteen nations, suggested that Nugan Hand was a firm of great success and repute. Michael stood silently for a moment, as if conjuring up a prayer, just as he had at the start of previous sessions. But this time his piercing blue eyes gradually hinted mischievous intent.

In a rich Bronx drawl, he roared: 'Hey troops, I want to thank you all again for coming down to Sydney!'

The delegates whooped and whistled in delight until Michael held up his hand and silence returned.

'From what we've discussed over the past days, I'd have to say the firm is well placed for a record year. Of course, much of our success is due to Frank Nugan.'

Mike scanned the delegates. 'Where the hell is Frank?'

George Shaw, a round-faced Lebanese-Australian staffer, hurried over to the door. At the end of the dimly lit corridor, he could make out the figure of Frank Nugan, leaning against a wall, trying to light a Cuban cigar with a recalcitrant lighter.

'Come on Frank, Mike's started.'

To enthusiastic applause, Frank appeared at the door, smiling and waving his Cuban in the air like a big shot and looking a million dollars in his high-sheen, silver-grey suit. As he took a seat in the front row, Admiral 'Buddy' Yates, a genial, bald-headed American in his mid-sixties, leaned forward and gave him an encouraging pat on the back.

'In the beginning,' Michael continued, 'Frank Nugan was the one with the technical expertise and I was the salesman. Isn't that right Frank?'

'That's how it was, Mike. That's how it was, for sure.'

'Now, I'm the pen pusher and Frank has turned into Dale Carnegie!'[1]

The delegates laughed as Frank expelled a cloud of cigar smoke.

'Frank's made us a great deal of money out of tax avoidance and that has underpinned our expansion. As the brochure says, Nugan Hand is now a global enterprise with a billion-dollar turnover. Only the Good Lord knows where we'll be in another seven years. But if they have money in the Afterlife, Nugan Hand International will be there! God Bless!'

As a staffer corralled the delegates together for a group photograph, Frank piped in, 'I just want to remind everyone what I said yesterday. The dough is not ours, okay? We'll go to jail if one dollar is missing — right? We are wealthy, handsome guys who wouldn't look good in arrows ... okay?'[2]

The delegates smiled nervously as the camera flash froze the moment for posterity.

*

Despite the brash opulence and optimism on display at the conference, the Nugan Hand financial empire was a house of cards buckling under the weight of its own ambition and ineptitude. Most of its international executives were former career military officers or ex-CIA, including Michael Hand. Remarkably, only one senior executive had prior banking experience.

Just three months after the conference, it all came tumbling down when the police discovered Frank Nugan dead in his Mercedes Benz, with a bullet in his brain and a military rifle in his lap. The police declared that Nugan had taken his own life. But items found in the car linking the bank to dozens of drug traffickers and to William Colby, the former director of the CIA, suggested something sinister was at play.

The NSW attorney-general, Frank Walker, called in his Corporate Affairs Commission investigators. On arrival at Nugan Hand's Sydney office, they walked into a crime scene. Most of the bank's records had either been destroyed or hurriedly moved to secret locations across the city in the dark of night.

A dozen international and Australian investigations ensued. When stories appeared in newspapers linking the bank to drug traffickers and the CIA, Michael Hand disappeared. His lawyer suggested to reporters that he had been abducted and possibly murdered. Homicide police believed otherwise. In July 1980, they issued a warrant for Hand's arrest for attempting to pervert the course of justice. Fearing that he may have skipped the country, they asked Interpol to make inquiries in the United States. But Michael Hand had vanished into the ether and hasn't been seen since.

★

With its cast of shady characters, the Nugan Hand saga played out like a political thriller, whose plotline ultimately splintered into a number of seemingly unsolvable mysteries. One writer suggested that Frank Nugan's death opened 'a can of worms, a mass of confusing strands from which the complete story almost certainly will never emerge.'[3]

When the story broke in 1980, I was enthralled by the fact that this international scandal was happening in my hometown of Sydney. I devoured every twist and turn but found it difficult to differentiate fact from speculation or conspiracy theory. Frustration peaked when, seven years later, the Royal Commission of Inquiry into the Activities of the Nugan Hand Group handed down its findings. The commission dismissed allegations that the bank was involved in drugs, gunrunning and CIA operations based on 'a lack of evidence'.

Three decades on, I felt that enough time had passed to revisit the case dispassionately to see what I could uncover. Perhaps there was a documentary to be made. As a starting point, I accessed the available investigation reports and interviewed on camera the surviving investigators and crime-busting politicians involved in the notorious case. Finding Nugan Hand staff willing to talk proved nigh on impossible, however. I traced the whereabouts of half a dozen people who worked for the bank. Some denied that they were the person I was trying to reach. Others promised to get back to me but never did. One high-ranking Nugan Hand executive threatened legal action if I dared even to mention his name. Another wanted to be helpful but became fearful that someone would identify him as the source.

It took two years to trace the owner of a bankbook found in Nugan's car. It turned out to be Michael Hand's driver, who had moved to Hollywood to work as an actor. He wouldn't talk either. Such reactions suggested that there was still information out there that could place people in danger.

Indeed, many people had since died, some in suspicious circumstances. These included an American-born bit player in the story who had assisted police investigators in return for immunity from prosecution. His wife told me that he had passed away unexpectedly on a visit back to the United States. She intimated that his death was suspicious and may have had something to do with Nugan Hand.

I also investigated the death of a former CIA pilot, Bud King, who had arrived in Australia with Michael Hand in 1967 to sell real estate in northern New South Wales. He died in Sydney in 1975. I learned that King's family back in America had been given two different stories about his death. His autopsy report revealed that neither version was true and that he had died in suspicious circumstances that were never properly investigated.

Eighteen months into my research I tracked down Doug Sapper, Michael Hand's Special Forces buddy in Vietnam. Sapper provided astonishing insights into the three main characters in the story: Michael Hand, Frank Nugan and Texas-born Kings Cross bar owner Bernie Houghton, who ended up running the bank's lucrative Middle East branches.

Sapper also revealed the bank's connections to intelligence agencies and Asian underworld groups, which were unknown at the time of the earlier investigations. And, in a surprising admission, Sapper told me of an extraordinary incident when associates of Houghton had asked him to travel to Sydney to carry out a murder.

Clearly, Nugan Hand was not some aberrant finance company operating in a vacuum and merely interested in ripping off millions of dollars from its customers. In Australia, the bank's operations crossed paths with dozens of major criminal cases, including a political assassination and the murder of two drug informants. On the world stage, Nugan Hand set itself up in major drug-trafficking hubs and areas of Cold War tension. It was as if Nugan Hand had deliberately positioned itself at the unholy nexus where organised crime and clandestine operations merge.

While the Australian investigators had unearthed some extraordinary linkages, they had also found a number of official doors closed to them. By accessing, through Freedom of Information, thousands of pages of documents from the FBI, US Department of State, ASIO and other government bodies I discovered how the Nugan Hand bank story had hit a raw nerve in US-intelligence and law-enforcement circles and caused diplomatic headaches, which I traced all the way to the White House.

*

When I embarked on this project, I hoped to discover the origins of this unique international scandal. To achieve that end, I needed to understand why Nugan died and why Michael Hand had disappeared. I set about creating a timeline of the Nugan Hand story, complete with episodes uncovered by the original investigations, and then researched the holes and imponderables in the timeline. Throughout the story there were dozens of actions taken by Nugan or Hand that left investigators bewildered. These included Hand's surprise resignation from the bank eighteen months after it began and Frank Nugan's ultimatum to his staff three months before his death to rid the bank of its illegal operations. Thirty-five years later, those mysteries are no longer mysteries.

And as for the greatest mystery of all, Michael Hand's whereabouts? He hasn't been seen since he fled Sydney in 1980.

I had read enough of the various inquiry reports to know that he was cunning and capable of extreme menace. I knew that if I ever traced Hand, he would be uncooperative. That said, I made numerous attempts to find him without success. Clearly, he had changed his name, and possibly his face, to evade detection.

As I neared completion of the first draft of this book, I made one final attempt to uncover his whereabouts. In a matter of hours, amongst a labyrinth of false trails, a path unexpectedly revealed itself, leading to a small, isolated town half a world away, where the darkest episode from Hand's past merged with his unfulfilled dream for the future of the Nugan Hand empire.

Even a highly-skilled CIA officer trained in the art of disappearance must appreciate that one fateful day someone could still trace him and announce, 'Time's up.' For Michael Hand, one of the world's most elusive corporate fugitives, that day has arrived.

1

WATCH OUT FOR THE CROCODILES

Standing atop of a rickety 10-metre-high tower in early 1964, Douglas A Sapper III, a twenty-one-year-old tough nugget of a man from Mount Vernon, Illinois, felt like the King of the World. The State of Georgia sure looked green and inviting from up there. On a clear night, they said, you could see the lights of Atlanta, more than 160 kilometres to the north.

When his trainer yelled, 'Jump!' there was no time for regrets. On the way down, Sapper just prayed that the parachute harness on his back would maintain its intimate relationship with the cable. This was only jump school at Fort Benning; a war zone was going to offer up far more hazards, including the likelihood of enemy fire. But he had joined up for exactly that kind of challenge.

It was during parachute training that Sapper met New York-born Michael Hand. Five-ten, with steel blue-eyes and a crazy laugh, Michael was buffed and handsome — the image of the all American boy.

'We were in the same class and we bonded,' Sapper later recalled. 'We were like birds of a feather. We realised, without statements on either side, that we were going to be professional soldiers.'[11]

Michael had been born into war. By Sapper's calculation, Michael's mother would have gone into labour during the Japanese attack on

Pearl Harbor. The following day, 8 December 1941, as President Roosevelt announced the declaration of war, Michael made his entry into the world.

His father, Oscar, was a clerk with the Department of Finance. The family lived in an apartment on Walton Avenue in the Bronx, one of New York's five boroughs, which had been taken over during the Prohibition years by bootleggers and gangs and gone into serious decline by the 1950s. On leaving school, Michael enrolled in a one-year course at the New York State Ranger School. After only nine months there he moved to California, and for most of 1960 managed a sports school in Los Angeles. In May 1963, Michael enlisted in the army. Following basic training, he was selected for Special Forces training with the elite Green Berets.

Despite their youth, life had already delivered both recruits a first-hand appreciation of mortality. In Doug Sapper's graduation year, while driving his father's Cadillac, he ran into a thirteen-year-old local boy who was riding a bicycle. The impact of the crash catapulted the boy into the windshield of the car and his body remained on the car as it skidded and crashed into a power pole. The boy died at the scene.

The year Michael Hand graduated from De Witt-Clinton High, his mother, Sally, fell to her death from the family's apartment window. Michael rarely spoke of his mother and Sapper sensed that it was not a subject he should raise:

> Michael did not advertise his background, or that his mother had killed herself, or accidentally fell off a balcony. I know that Michael went to several different educational institutions and gravitated to join the army and never looked back. In fact, throughout military training the thing you noticed about Michael was that he was driven.[2]

Hand and Sapper were indoctrinated in the art of unconventional warfare at Fort Bragg in North Carolina:

> When you were selected for Special Forces training, you could pretty much look people in the eye and say, 'I'm one of the chosen few.' We weren't boy scouts. This wasn't a church camp. We were trained to go in and destroy things. Michael did not have an aversion to closing the distance with another human being and he was the kind of guy people wanted on their Special Forces team. Michael looked good in a uniform. He had that prize-winning smile and that twinkle in his eye. But he was also the kind of guy who looked for loyalty, bravery and commitment. One of the things that bonded us was a rash of spinal meningitis going through that training cycle. There had already been one soldier die from it. We were in the barracks one night when one of the trainees had convulsions and started foaming at the mouth and fell on the floor. Everybody thought it was meningitis and so I tried to help him and I told everybody to get out of the barracks and Michael stayed and we attended that kid until the ambulance came. I think at that point there was a bond there. We knew that no matter how deep the shit got, he and I would still be standing there. And that was the beginning of a long, long friendship.[3]

In February 1965, they arrived in Tay Ninh Province, Vietnam. That month, the United States began its campaign of sustained bombing raids of North Vietnam, dubbed Operation Rolling Thunder:

> In the background of everybody's mind was the knowledge that being in a Special Forces camp in Vietnam was hazardous. One of the worst fears was of the camp being over-run and so

you didn't want a bunch of guys who were really adept at opening a tuna fish can but didn't have their shit together to defend you. Michael was a radio operator, he was a good teammate and everybody knew that Michael Hand, when push came to shove, could be seriously dangerous.[4]

In early June 1965, Hand was dispatched to a camp at Dong Xoai, 100 kilometres northeast of Saigon. Manned by four hundred Montagnard troops and nineteen Special Forces and US Navy construction specialists called Seabees, the camp sat at the end of the Ho Chi Min trail — a choke point for the Vietnamese Communists trying to move into South Vietnam. In such a strategic location it was never a question of 'will we be attacked?', only a question of 'when?'

Just before midnight on 9 June 1965, explosions rocked the camp. Michael Hand recalled that night in an army radio broadcast:

> When the initial mortar barrage started at quarter to twelve, there was so much screaming and confusion and death in the immediate vicinity; everybody tried to do the most sensible thing in dispersing themselves around our perimeter wall. Everybody had their individual weapons as well as the crew-type weapons. For the first two hours of the battle, heavy mortar, machine guns, small arms and Chinese rifles were used against us. The Americans in the compound, which included the Special Forces and the Seabee attachment, dispersed themselves along the wall and tried to give them a good volume of fire to hold down the North Vietnamese who were attacking us. Two hours in, the VC hit us with flamethrowers as well as an increased barrage of fire.[5]

As the intense onslaught of mortars and recoilless rifle rounds, grenades and flame-throwers hammered the camp, fifteen hundred Viet Cong guerrillas moved in and overwhelmed the defenders. Hurtling through a gauntlet of razor wire and enemy rounds, Hand and four of his comrades withdrew to the district chief's compound on the other side of the camp. So began one of the first major battles of the Vietnam War.

Doug Sapper was on reconnaissance mission elsewhere, but happened to be on radio watch when Dong Xoai was hit:

> The first mortar round took out one of their radios and the next mortar round went through the team-house roof and I don't remember all the people that it wounded or killed but the Viet Cong got inside the wire almost immediately and it was a very bloody, intense, right-up-close-and-personal battle. They killed or wounded many of the American defenders. Michael, along with the executive officer of the team, Lieutenant Williams, held that team together in defence. It was so intense it was like the defenders of the Alamo; they had to drop back, drop back, drop back. In the last hour or so of the battle, they ended up in the inside of an artillery pit and they were running out of ammunition. At that point, Mike had already been fighting for forty-eight hours.[6]

The last radio still operating at Dong Xoai sent out a desperate plea for support: 'I am using my last battery for the radio and there is no more ammunition; we are all wounded, some of the more serious are holding grenades with the safety pins already pulled. The VC are attacking in human waves. The last wave has been defeated, but we are expecting the next wave now.'[7]

Sapper scrambled aboard one of the three helicopters that departed on the rescue mission into Dong Xoai:

I was with what they call an extraction team or a hatchet force, to go in and try to get fighters into the camp to reinforce these guys. We couldn't get near it. We got shot off the LZ [landing zone]. By this time, Michael was out of bullets and, realising that death was probably just minutes away, he had a psychotic break. All he had was his Ka-bar knife. He mutilated quite a few of them with that. One of the VC grabbed him and Michael stabbed him and ripped the knife up through his sternum and the guy hit the ground and Michael put his foot on the guy's leg and grabbed his head and literally lifted it up and separated his head from his body. That was a Kodak moment. Yes, he tore the guy's head completely off his body ... I don't know if the Viet Cong or the North Vietnamese Army that attacked the camp that night knew his name, but I guarantee after that they remembered Michael because he killed a truckload of them. It was his finest hour.[8]

Mounting a second desperate rescue mission, US military helicopters successfully landed on the Dong Xoai soccer field. Hand had been hit twice by mortar shrapnel but, before evacuating, volunteered to go back and retrieve another wounded comrade. As the choppers departed, the area was hit by mortar fire and raked by large-calibre machine guns. Only six of the nineteen Americans survived. All were wounded.

Just by the grace of God, Michael and several other people were able to escape. Michael came to Saigon to the Third Field Hospital. No major wounds, but just a thousand little wounds, basically small pieces of shrapnel that had embedded in his skin. I stayed at the hospital to take care of Michael while he was recovering. If you were to ask me did I think that transformed Michael, I think that would transform just about anybody. You pull somebody's head off their body and blood is squirting up about a foot over their shoulders, now that would transform you. He was pretty screwed up. I mean, he thought he was going to die, and he was just going to take as many of these people with him as he possibly could. He just became a robot, just went nuts; that is one of the reasons he survived. There are stories that he killed twenty guys with his bare hands.[9]

During the battle Hand risked his life to retrieve four wounded men. He was awarded the Distinguished Service Cross (DSC), the military's second highest award for heroism. Following his discharge from hospital, he was reassigned to the John F Kennedy Center for Special Warfare at Fort Bragg, North Carolina, where he received special instruction from CIA paramilitary officers for another mission — something completely off the radar.*

Doug Sapper saw it as a natural development for someone like Hand, who was unshaken in his belief that his country was on the side of right in the Vietnam War: 'In Special Forces there wasn't anything we couldn't accomplish. You give us a mission; we'll get it done. And Michael was a product of that environment. So when Michael got out of the military, he went to work for the Central Intelligence Agency. It was the next step.'[10]

After three months of intensive training, the CIA loaded Mike onto a Continental Air Services transport bound for Laos on a top-secret mission dubbed 'Project 404'. Laos was a neutral country, but in 1965 intelligence reports warned Washington that Vietnamese communist forces were spilling over the border into Laos. By the time Mike Hand arrived, Laos was in the thick of the largest covert

---

* During the Vietnam War, Special Forces followed the protocols of the military, but in reality the CIA called the shots. The CIA funded their missions, helped build their camps and directed their missions.

military operation in the CIA's history. He was assigned to a group called 'Requirements Organization', training Hmong hill tribesmen in the dark arts of counterinsurgency to oppose the North Vietnamese–backed Pathet Lao communists.

According to Doug Sapper, being in Laos was like being in a war that didn't exist: 'I used to describe it as a place far, far away, populated by people that don't exist, where things never happened. And Michael got thrust into that. He taught the Hmong different things about communications, about weapons, demolitions, about ambushes and then sent them out on patrols.'[11]

In Laos, Mike Hand met CIA pilot Kermit Walker King, a willowy, forty-year-old with a hollow 'Gomer Pyle' grin and a gung-ho attitude, who went by the name 'Bud'. In a small, twin-engine, unarmed Piper Apache aircraft, King carried out night-time airdrops over the Ho Chi Minh Trail, directed Laotian strike planes to their targets and ferried men, weapons and provisions into mountainous, precarious locations.

King introduced Mike Hand to Paul Stocker, a big-shot American lawyer who'd served two terms in the Washington State Legislature in the 1950s. In a scenario befitting *Catch 22*, Stocker was travelling around Laos in the middle of a covert war selling blocks of coastal land in Australia to employees of Air America and the CIA. Stocker talked Bud and Mike into signing up to his real estate venture, not as buyers but as salesmen.

In late 1966, following his Laos service, Michael Hand returned to the United States. Wearing a crisp shirt, tie and tailored suit, he walked into the Australian consulate on New York's Fifth Avenue and was ushered into the office of an official named Waddell. Michael looked on as Waddell opened a large envelope and extracted a letter with a photograph of fingerprints attached.

'The New Jersey police say you're an upright citizen,' said Waddell, as he picked up Hand's visa application and scanned it.

Hand had stated that he had won a DSC and that after his service in Vietnam he'd worked for the US Government in 'communications'. With the stroke of a pen, and for the princely sum of a single dollar, the young American was given permanent residency in Australia. As Hand stood to leave, Waddell took one last scan of his application.

'You say here you are going to be looking for construction work in the Northern Territory?'

'Yes, Sir.'

'Tough country up there. Watch out for the crocodiles.' [12]

*

If Hand intended on settling in the Northern Territory, he got off at the wrong stop. In October 1967, he flew into Sydney and gravitated to King Cross, where the only evidence of reptilian life was the blue-tongued spruikers parading up and down outside the ubiquitous strip clubs.

Hand and King met with Paul Stocker at the newly opened Bourbon & Beefsteak Bar and Restaurant. Stocker handed them a bunch of glossy brochures and a sales script and told them to get to work. Coincidentally, or not, the first planeload of US servicemen on R&R from the Vietnam War had just arrived in Sydney. They were bussed to an R&R centre, where they were given a run-down of the city and told that Kings Cross was the ideal place to spend their week's leave. After partaking of the sexual services on offer around the Cross, the servicemen flocked to the 'Bourbon' for American home-style food and entertainment. Its forty-eight-year-old Texas-born proprietor, Bernie Houghton, was the perfect host. Bernie had run servicemen's bars in Saigon and Bangkok and seemed to have had foreknowledge of the US Government's choice of Sydney as its upcoming R&R hotspot for the US forces.

Detective Sergeant Clive Small probed Bernie Houghton's early years in Sydney:

> Houghton was one of the most mysterious characters that you would meet in Kings Cross in those days. He set up his business effectively in the months before approval was given for US military resources to come to Australia on R&R from the Vietnam War. You could be forgiven for suspecting that he knew something in advance and was taking advantage of it.[13]

With Bernie's blessing, Mike and Bud based themselves at the Bourbon & Beefsteak and started selling slices of paradise to young, impressionable GIs fresh from a war zone. The blocks on offer were part of a large coastal development in subtropical northern New South Wales, called 'Ocean Shores'. The scheme was bankrolled by a big American tycoon and boasted popular singer Pat Boone as its figurehead. The genius of working out of the Bourbon was that fresh groups of GIs and navy guys were arriving in Kings Cross every week. With every sale Mike and Bud earned a tidy 25 per cent commission.

In December 1968, Bud King returned to Laos and flew back two weeks later via Darwin in a Piper Apache aircraft he'd just purchased from Continental Air Service, a CIA airline. Bud figured that if any potential buyer proved a hard nut to crack, he would fly them up to Ocean Shores to seal the deal. A few weeks later, his Thai housekeeper, Arina, flew in from the Laotian capital, Vientiane, to help cater for buyers and dignitaries visiting Ocean Shores, including Pat Boone and Hollywood actor William Holden.

In 1970, Doug Sapper and an army buddy flew from Saigon to Sydney on R&R:

> We went down to Kings Cross — well of course everybody

talks about Kings Cross and we had heard about the Bourbon & Beefsteak, where all these GIs went, so we went down there. We saw the same GIs there every day on a five-day R&R. They didn't go on cruises of Sydney Harbour. They would spend almost all their time in that bar. Well, it was because they felt safe there. There was camaraderie there. There was an easy ear they could talk to — Bernie or one of his managers — and they could get things done. If someone said, 'Bernie, where can I get laid?' or 'Bernie, where can I get this?' he knew. So when they got back, it was 'How was Sydney?' 'I guess it's great man, that bar is really a hell of a place to be.' In that, you have to assume there was some illegal activity somewhere. Bars, alcohol, prostitution, some drugs, whatever — it all kind of fits in a package.[14]

At the Bourbon, Sapper learned to his astonishment that Michael Hand was living in Sydney. He called him up and went over to his home for dinner. The biggest surprise was that Mike had recently married a beautiful Australian woman — a former model, who worked for a flash Sydney jeweller.

Helene was her name. She was older than he was by about five or so years. A phenomenal woman, I mean a very strong personality but very supportive and extremely loyal. He married her within just a little over a year of arriving in Australia. It didn't take him long to fall under her spell, I guess you'd say. In a quiet moment I said to Michael, 'How the hell did you end up here?' When he left Laos I just assumed that he had returned to New York. He said he was selling some kind of real estate investment. I just said, 'Now that's a shift in direction.'[15]

Curious about his army buddy's transformation from war hero to salesman, Sapper headed back to the Bourbon on his last night in Sydney:

> There was Michael, perfectly tied tie, starched shirt, good-looking suit. He comes around the table and you could just tell this is Dale Carnegie — a sort of a super-salesman persona. He was getting all the right hook lines and getting all the right timing. He was magnetic. But he was a real estate salesman? I could tell that Michael was in survival mode, and he wasn't going to be satisfied with selling land down in this property development. He was looking for something that had a future.

www.ingramcontent.com/pod-product-compliance
Lightning Source LLC
Chambersburg PA
CBHW051537010526
44107CB00064B/2752